PERTH AND SURROUNDS

(in colour and black and white)

by Eli Zagoria

Perth in Western Australia is one of the most isolated cities in the world. It was built where the Swan and Canning Rivers meet and they flow to Fremantle, its adjoining port city.

On the west of Perth is the Indian Ocean and the city borders and is overlooked by a massive and green Kings Park.

Perth is relaxed with an easy going pace with long uncrowded beaches and sunshine. Its natural beauty makes it a popular tourist destination.

National Library of Australia Cataloguing-in-Publication entry
Author: Zagoria, Eli, 1922-2013, artist.
Title: Perth and surrounds (in colour and black and white)
              by Eli Zagoria / paintings by Eli Zagoria ;
              compiler David Solly Sandler.
ISBN: 9780992468408
Series: Eli Zagoria's art ; v. 6.
Subjects: Zagoria, Eli, 1922-2013.
              Artists--Western Australia,--20th century.
              Painting, Australian--Western Australia--Perth.
              Art--Western Australia--Perth.
              Flowers in art..
              Perth (W.A.) in art.
Other Authors/Contributors:
              Sandler, David Solly, compiler.

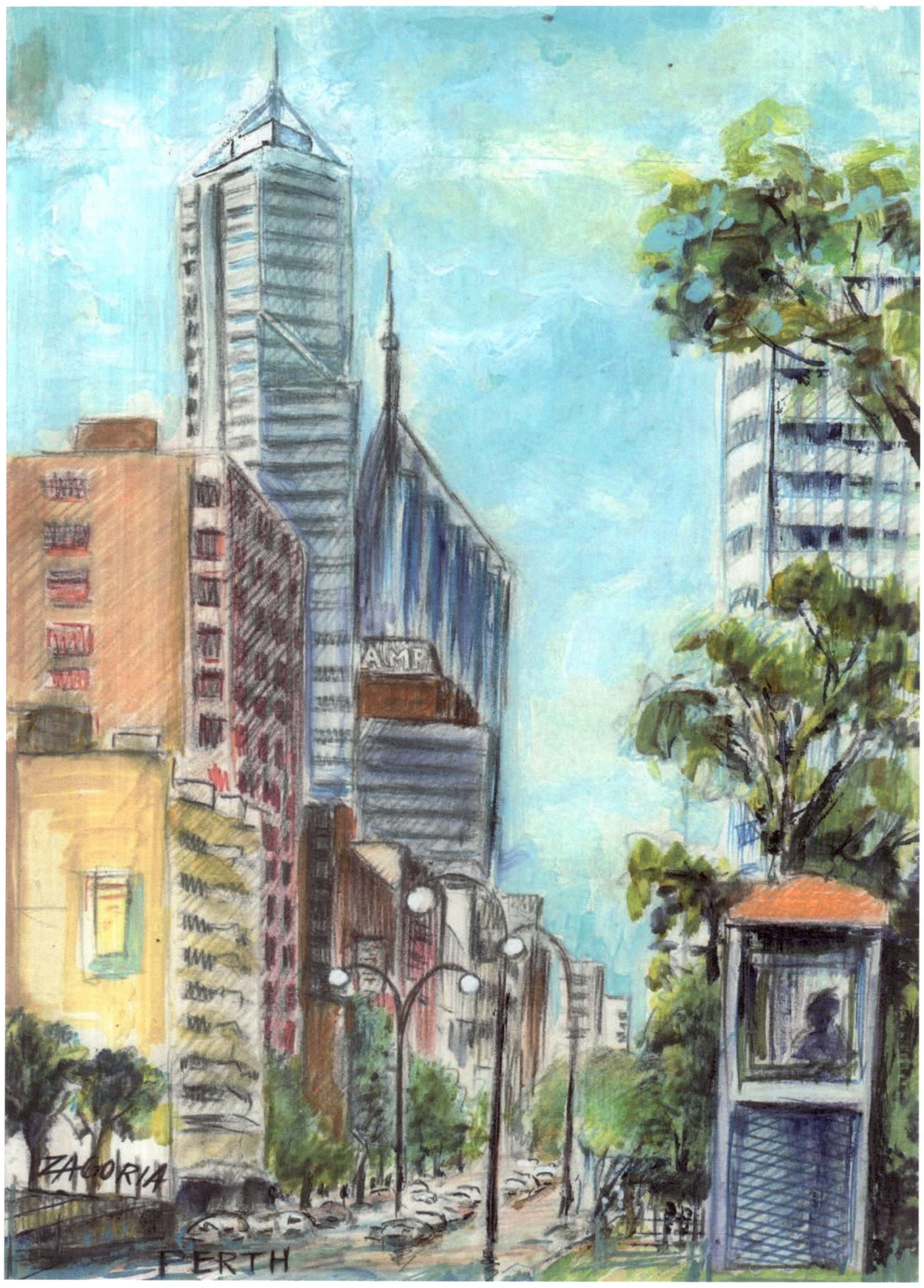

PERTH

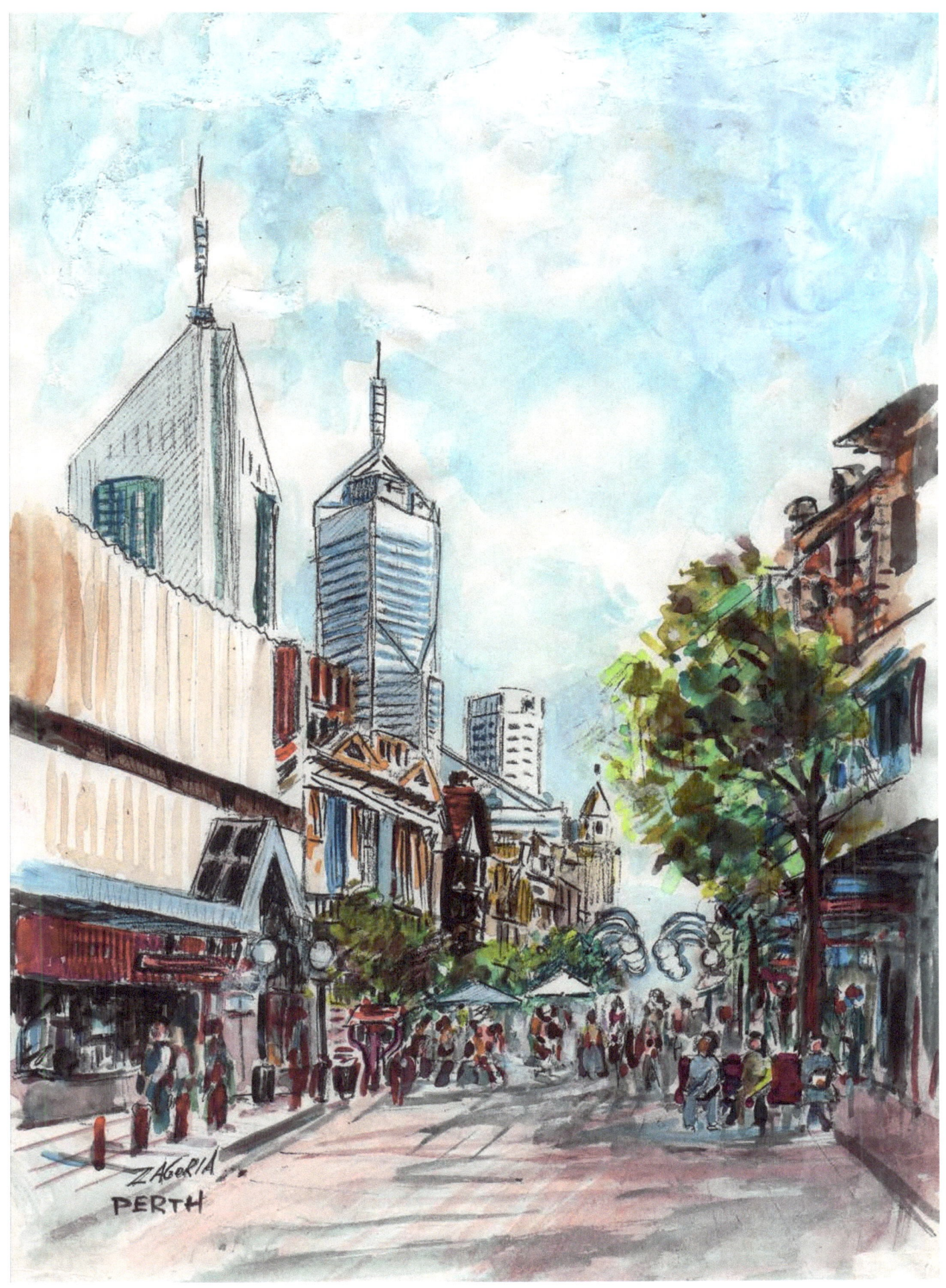

ZAGORIA
PERTH

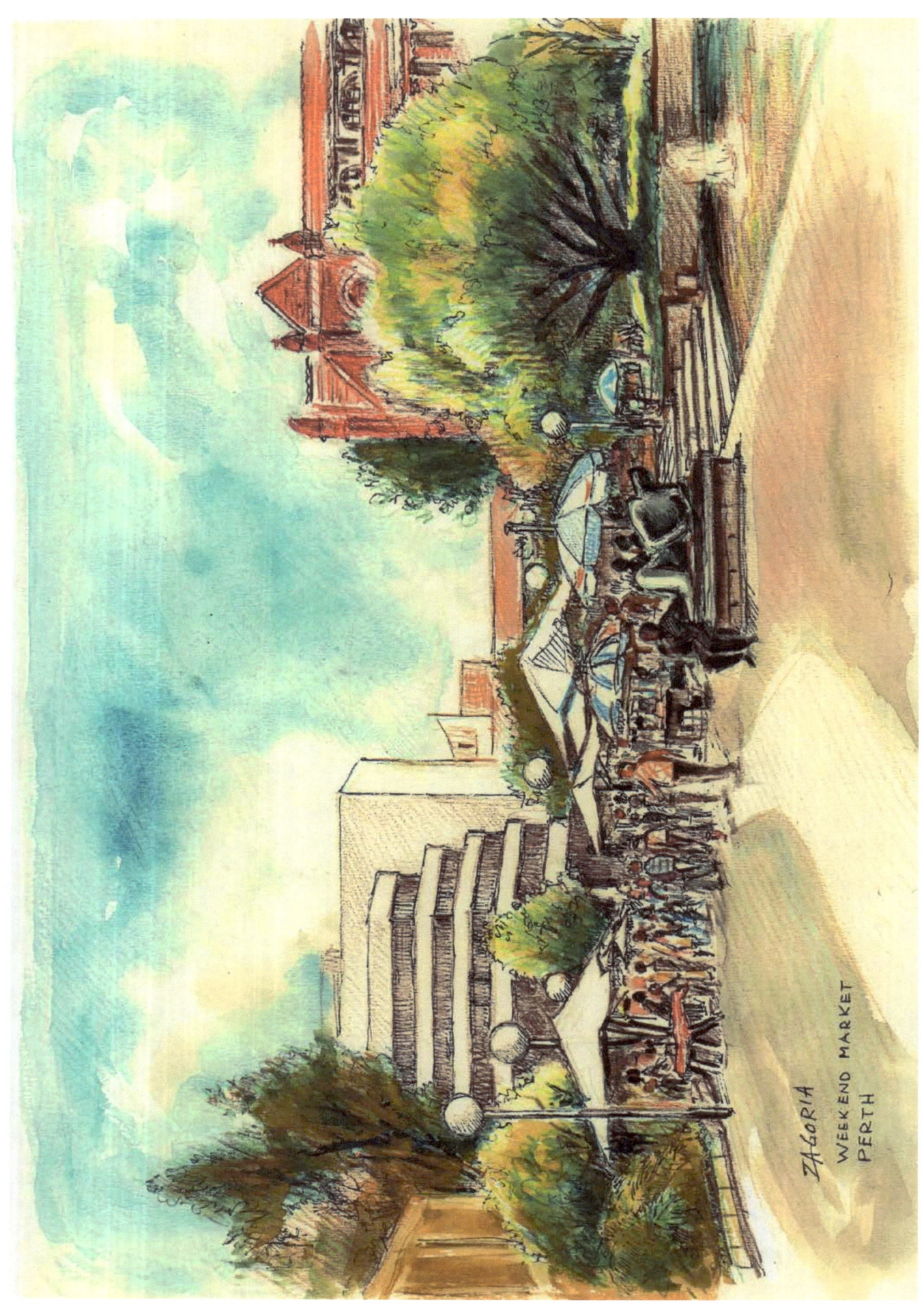

ZAGORIA

WEEKEND MARKET
PERTH

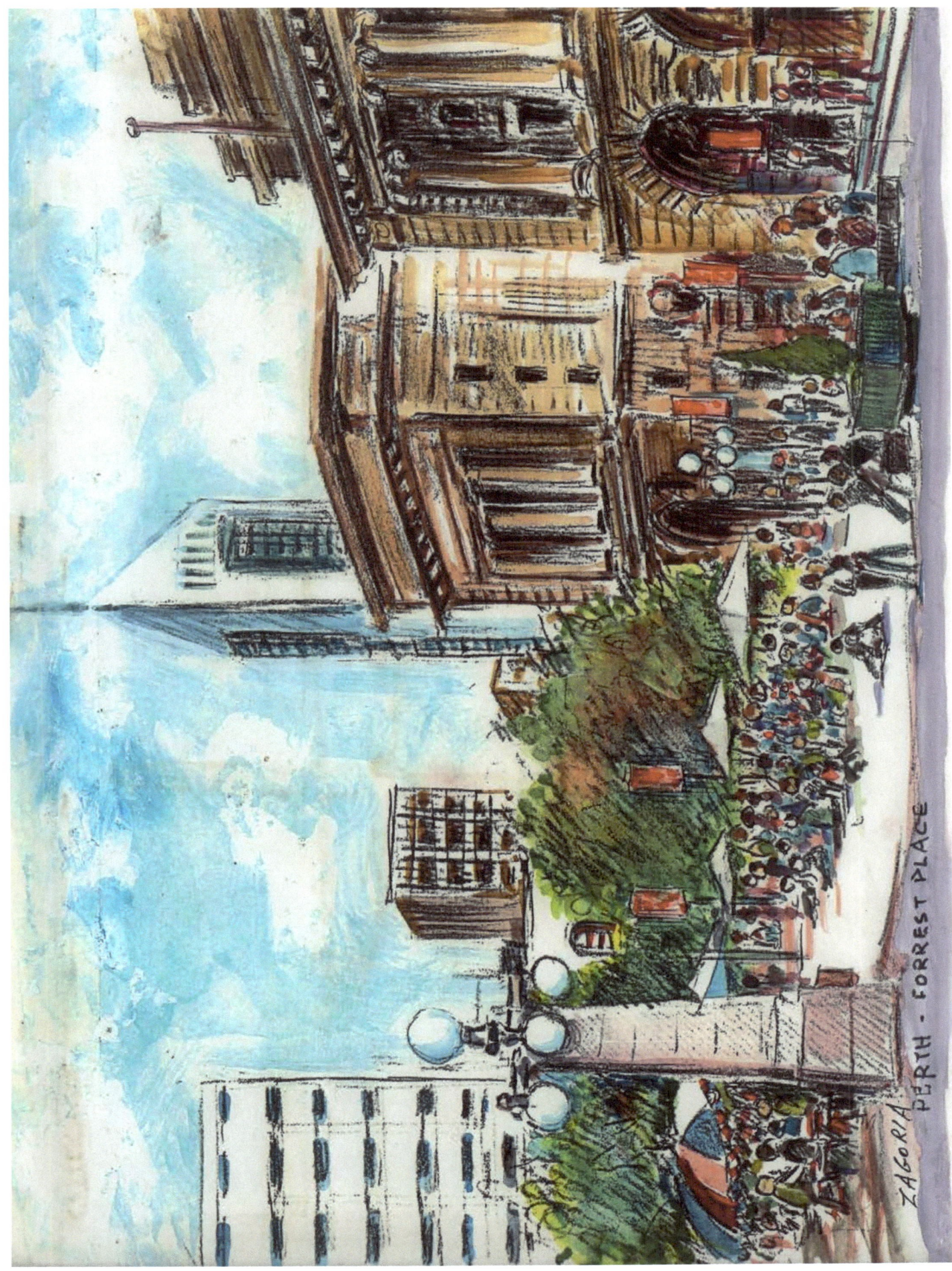

ZAGORIA

PERTH - FORREST PLACE

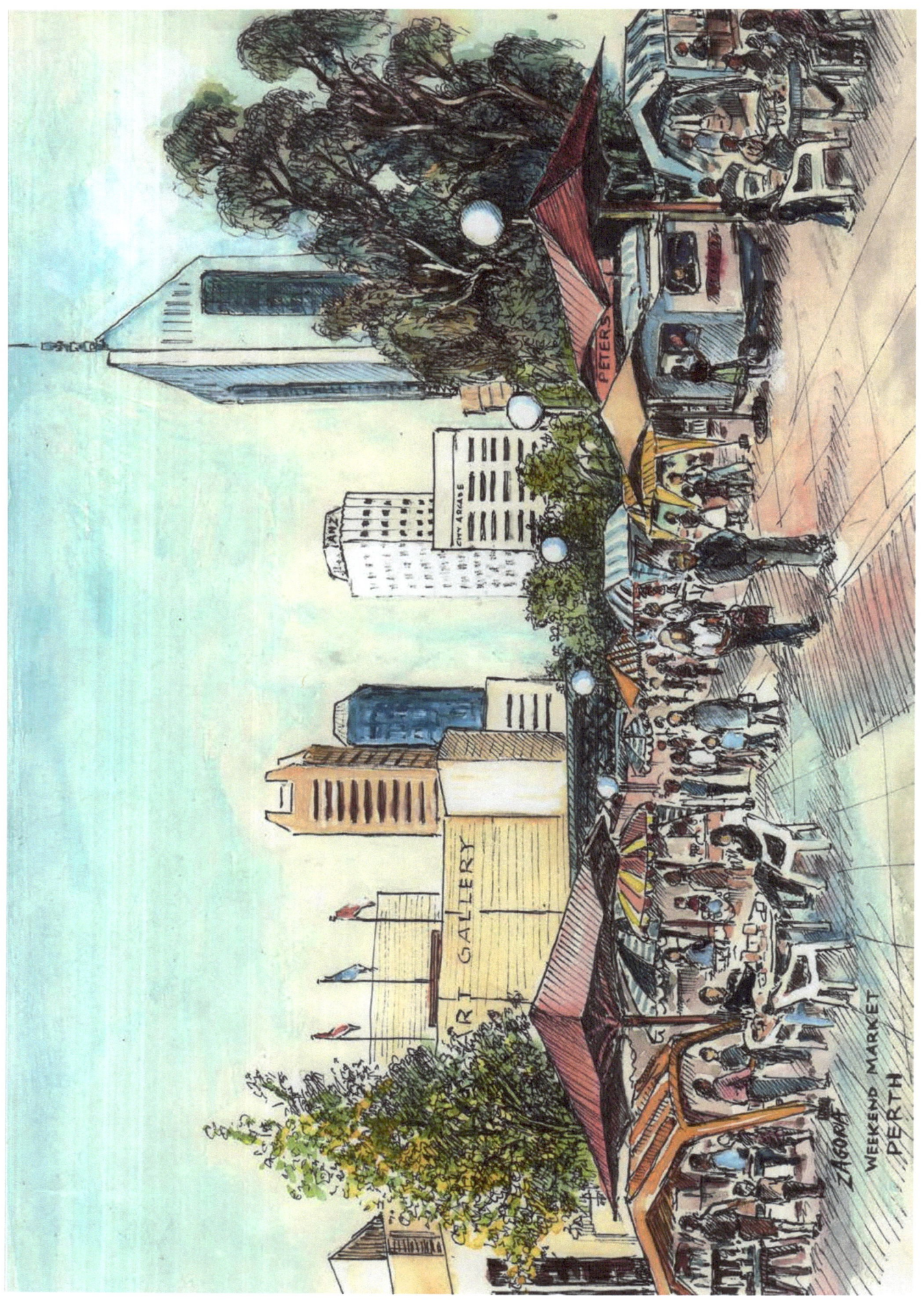

WEEKEND MARKET
PERTH

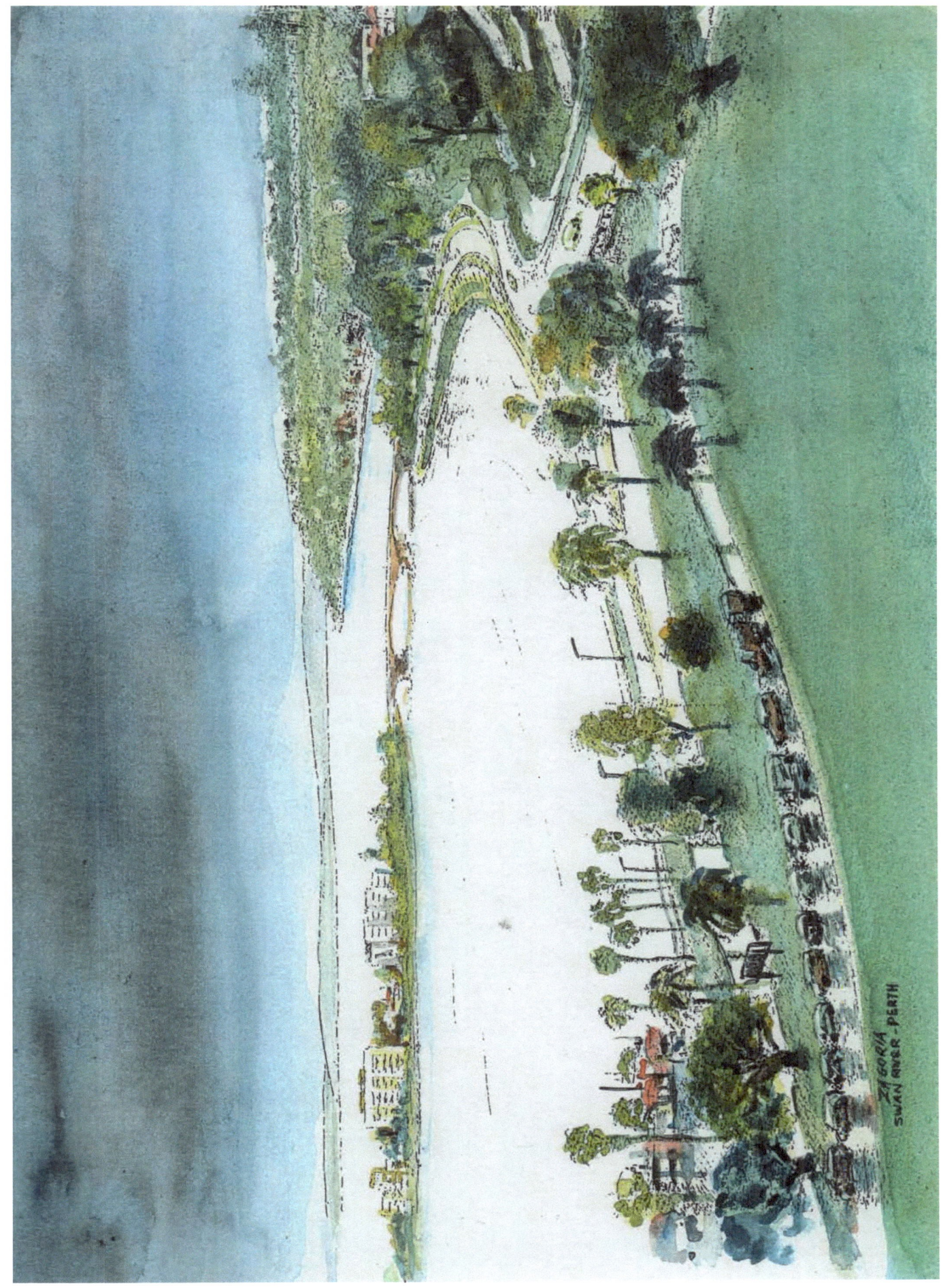

ZAGORIA
SWAN RIVER - PERTH

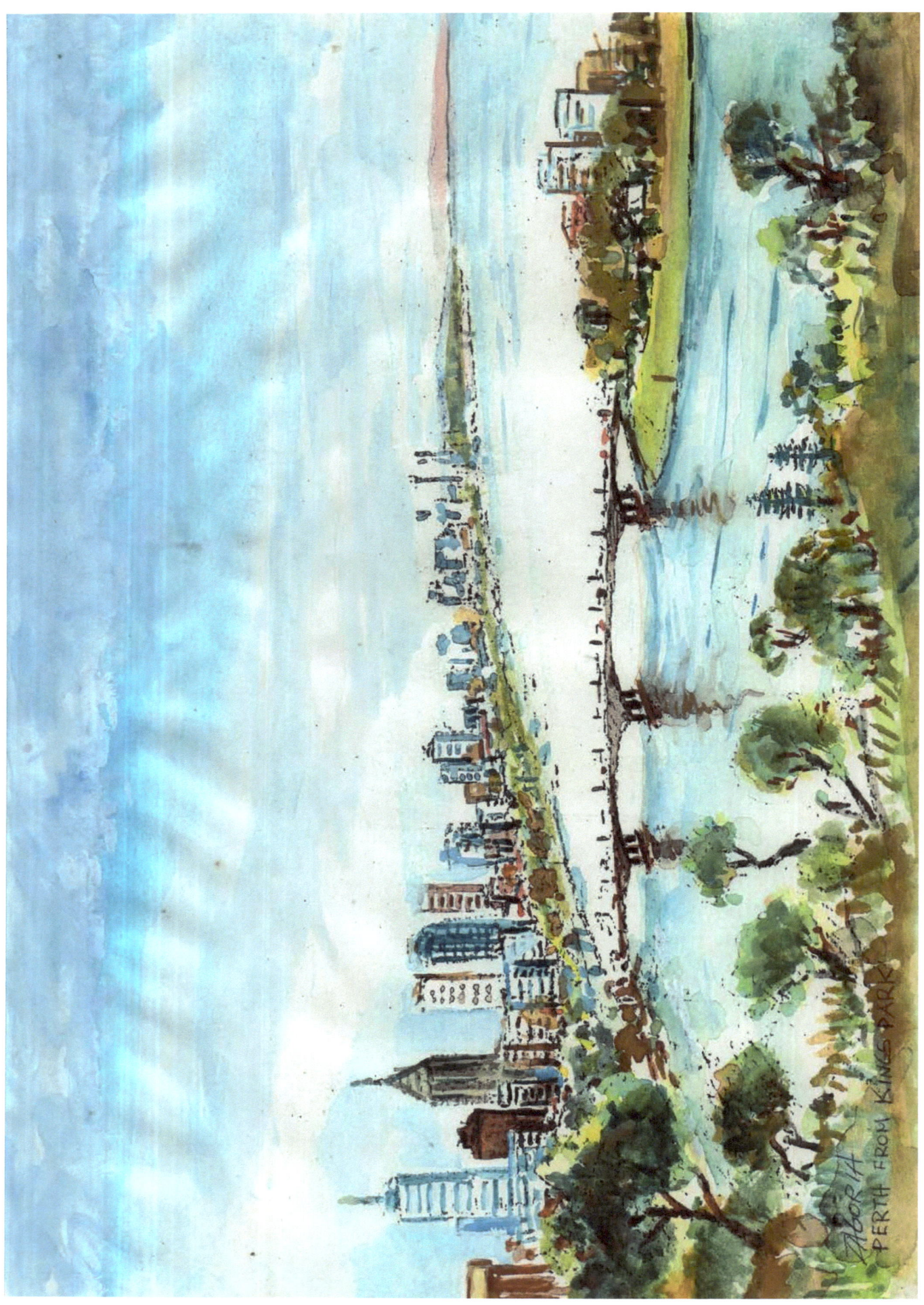

VICTORIA
PERTH FROM KINGS PARK

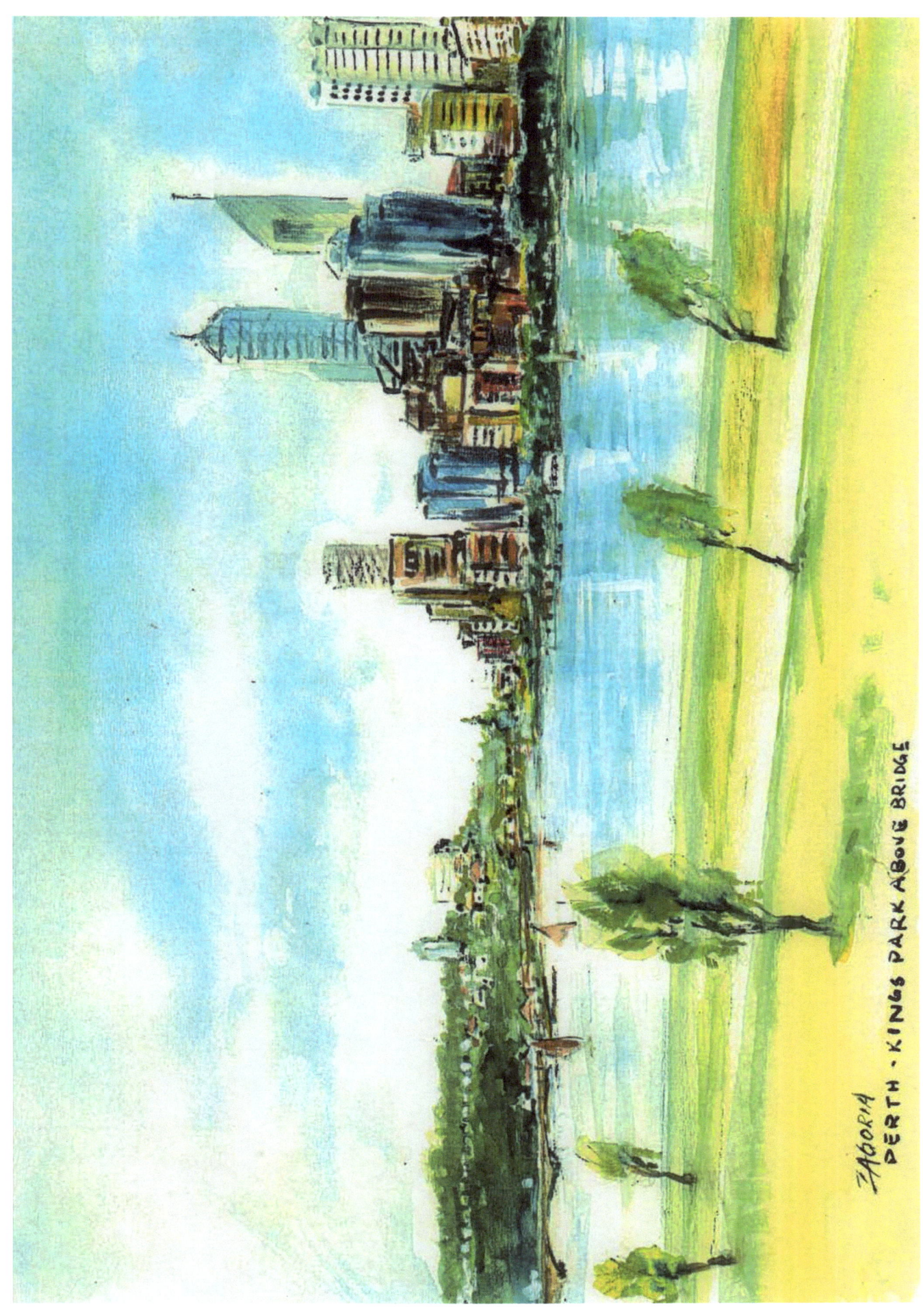

ZABORIA
PERTH - KINGS PARK ABOVE BRIDGE

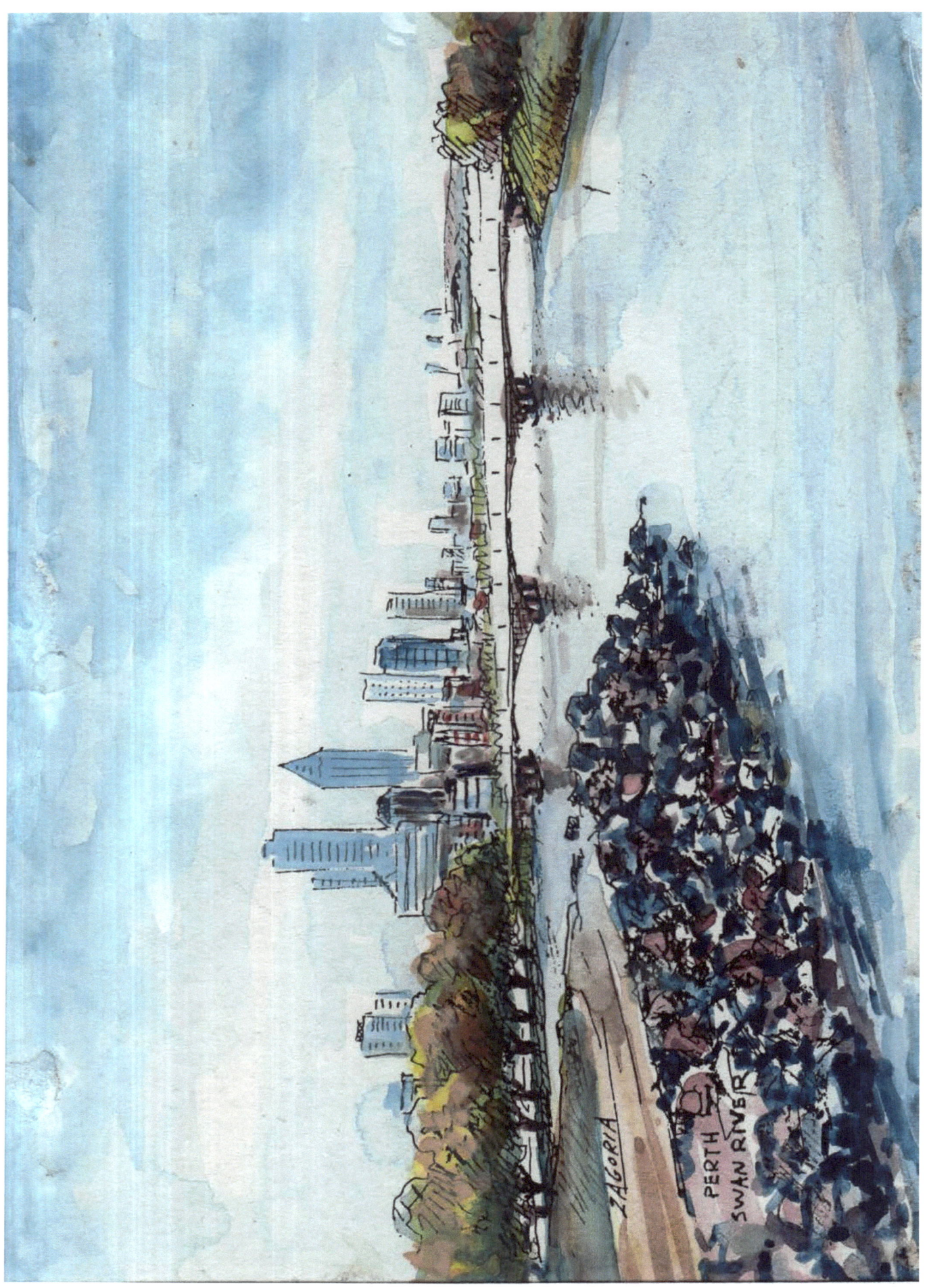

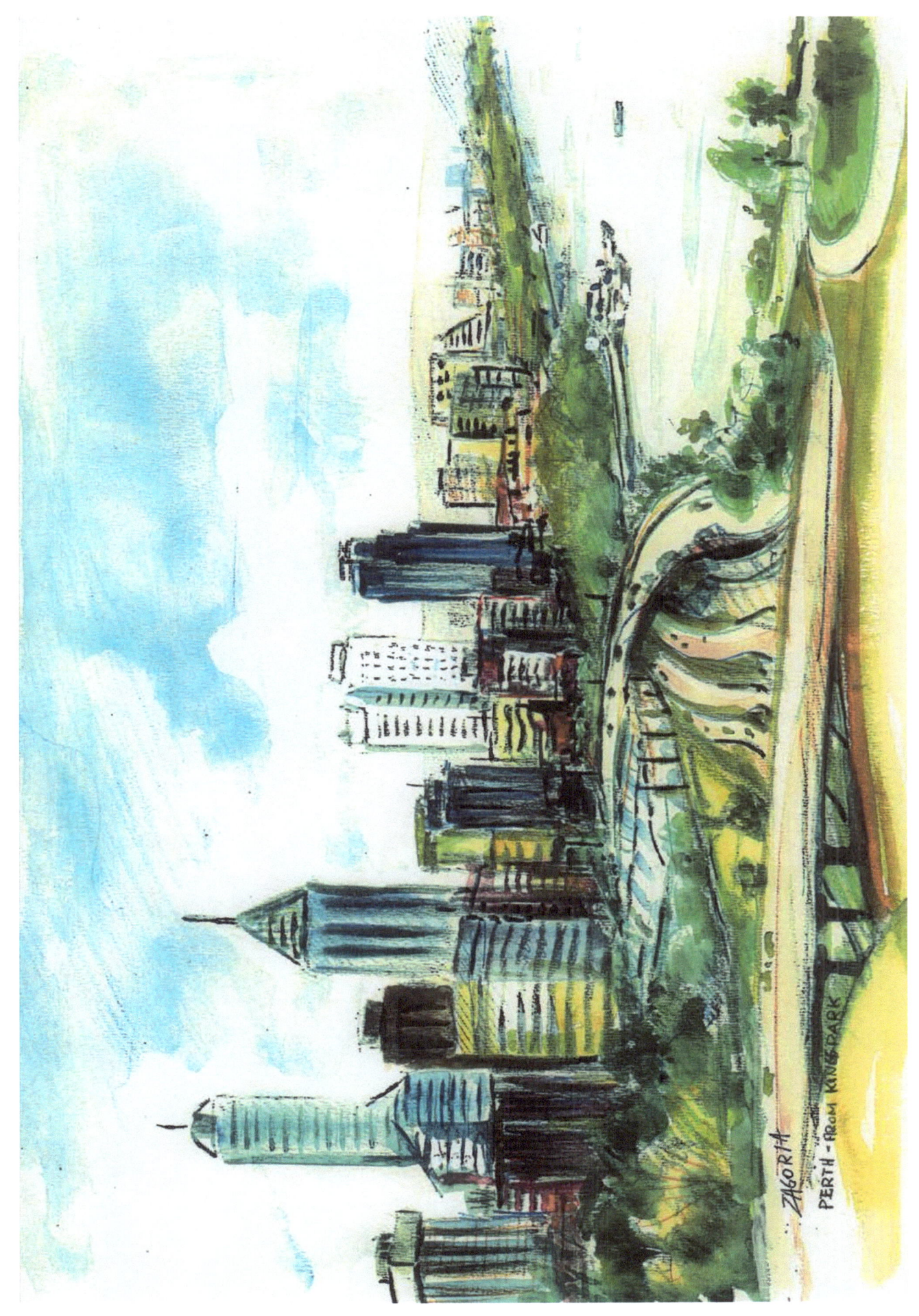

ZAGORIA

PERTH - FROM KINGS PARK

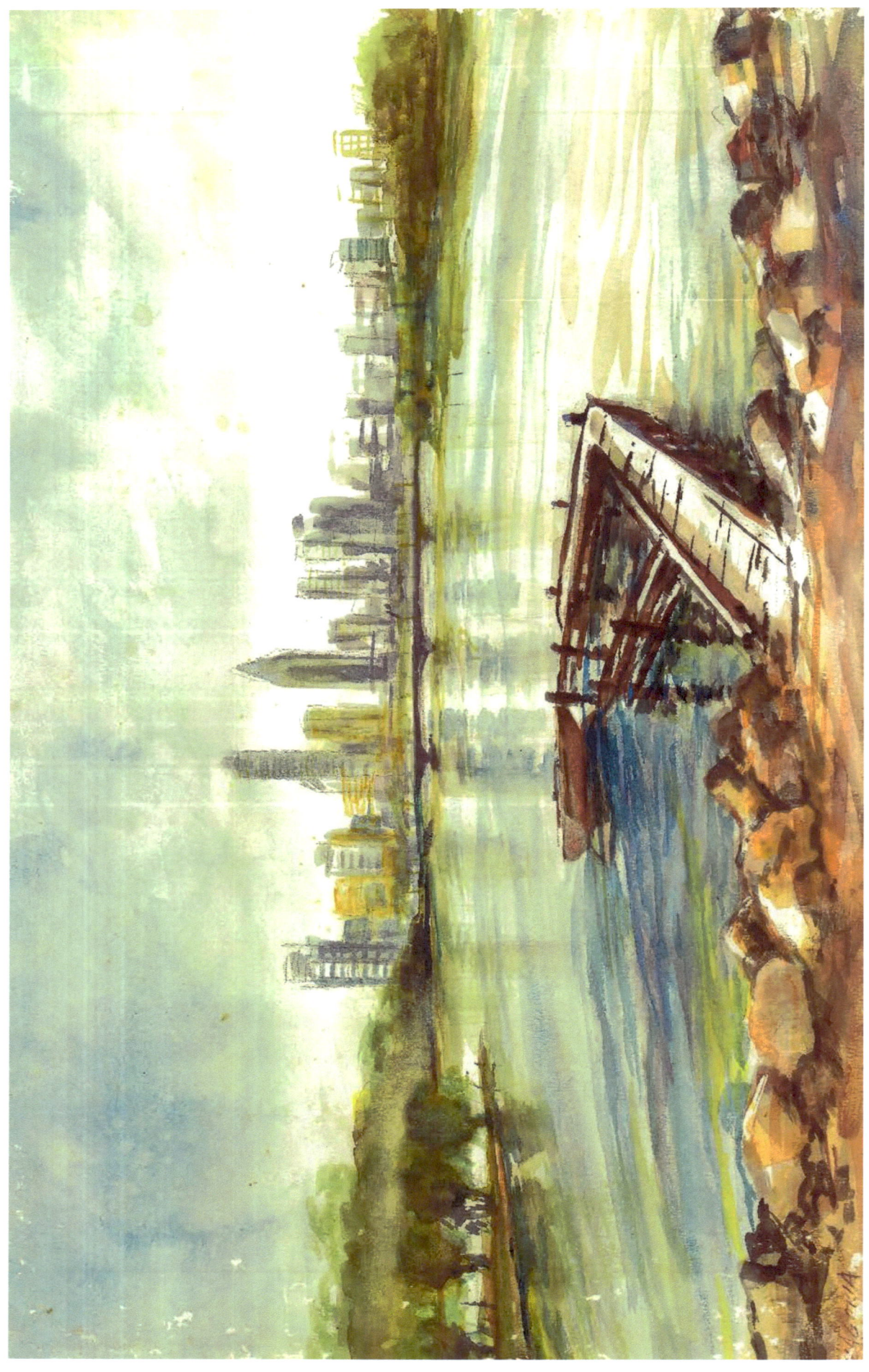

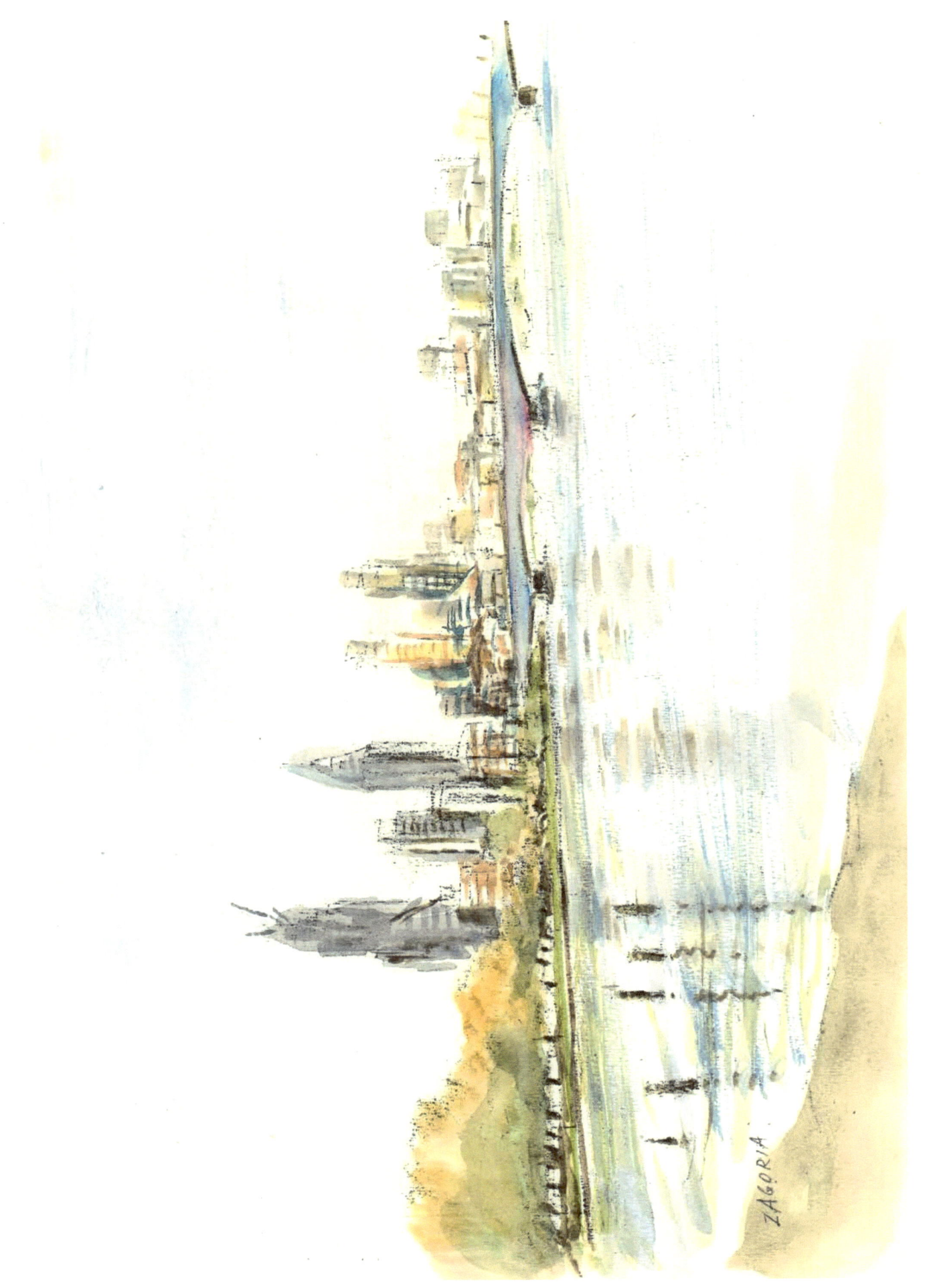

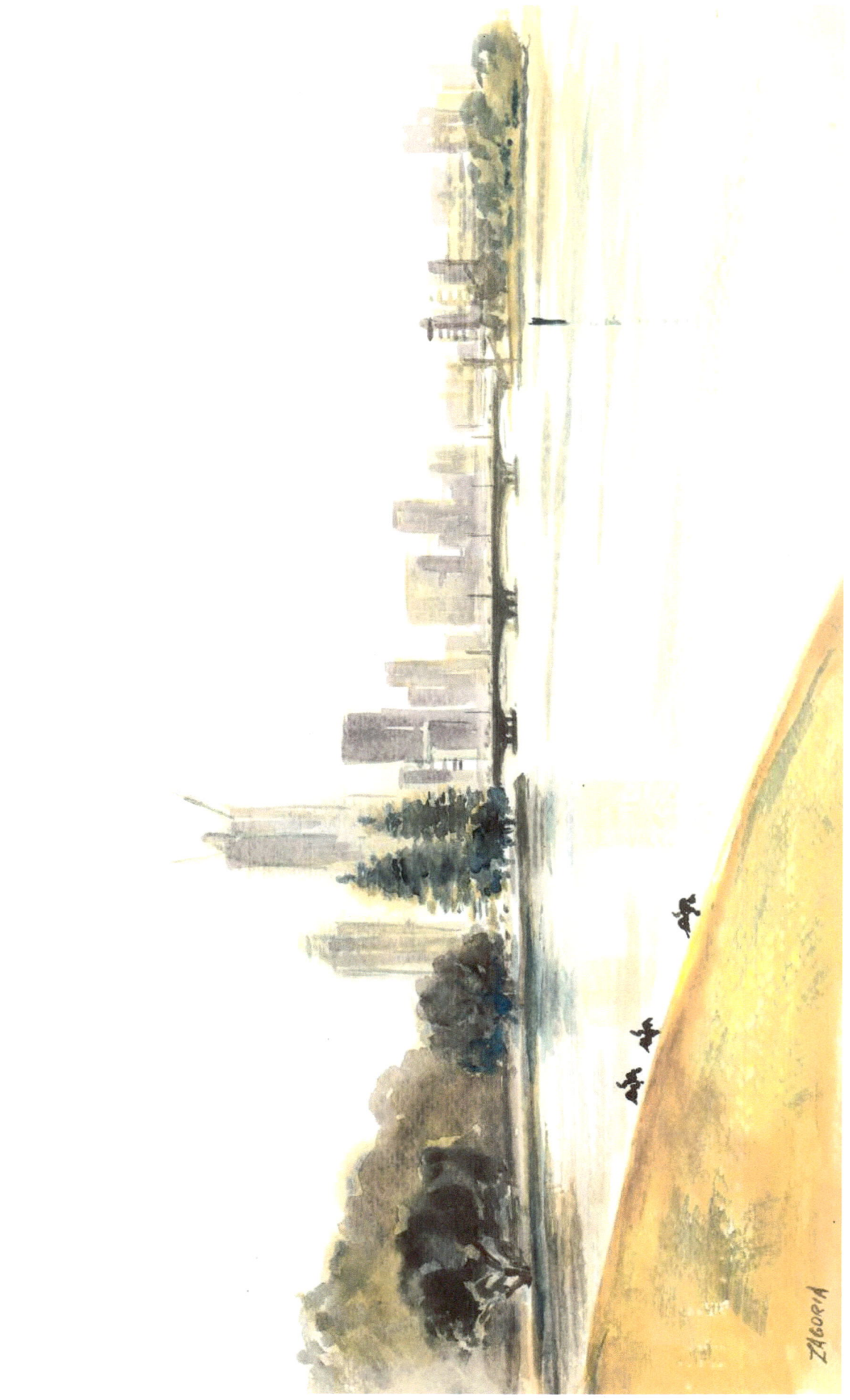

ZAGORIA

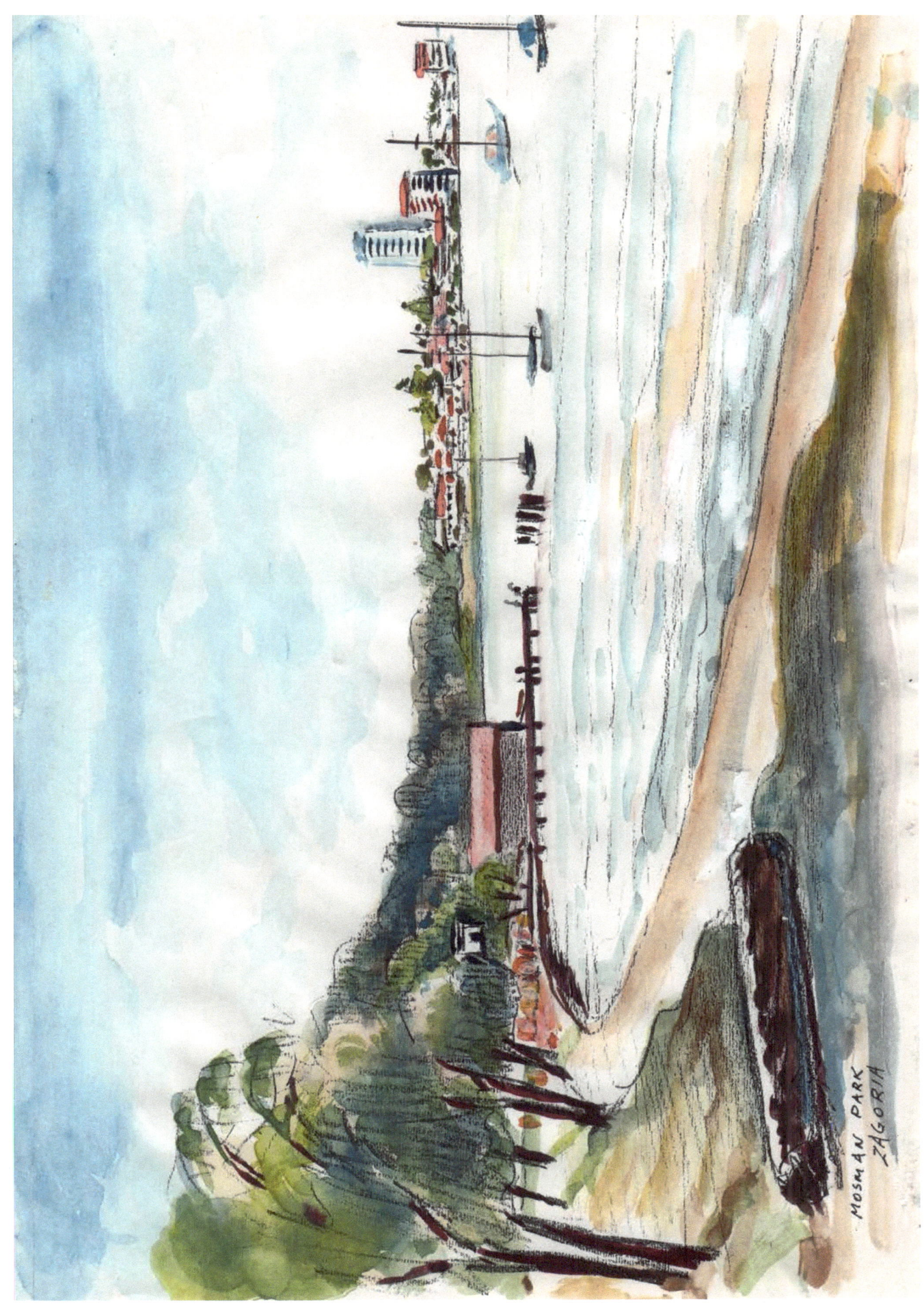

MOSMAN PARK
ZAGORIA

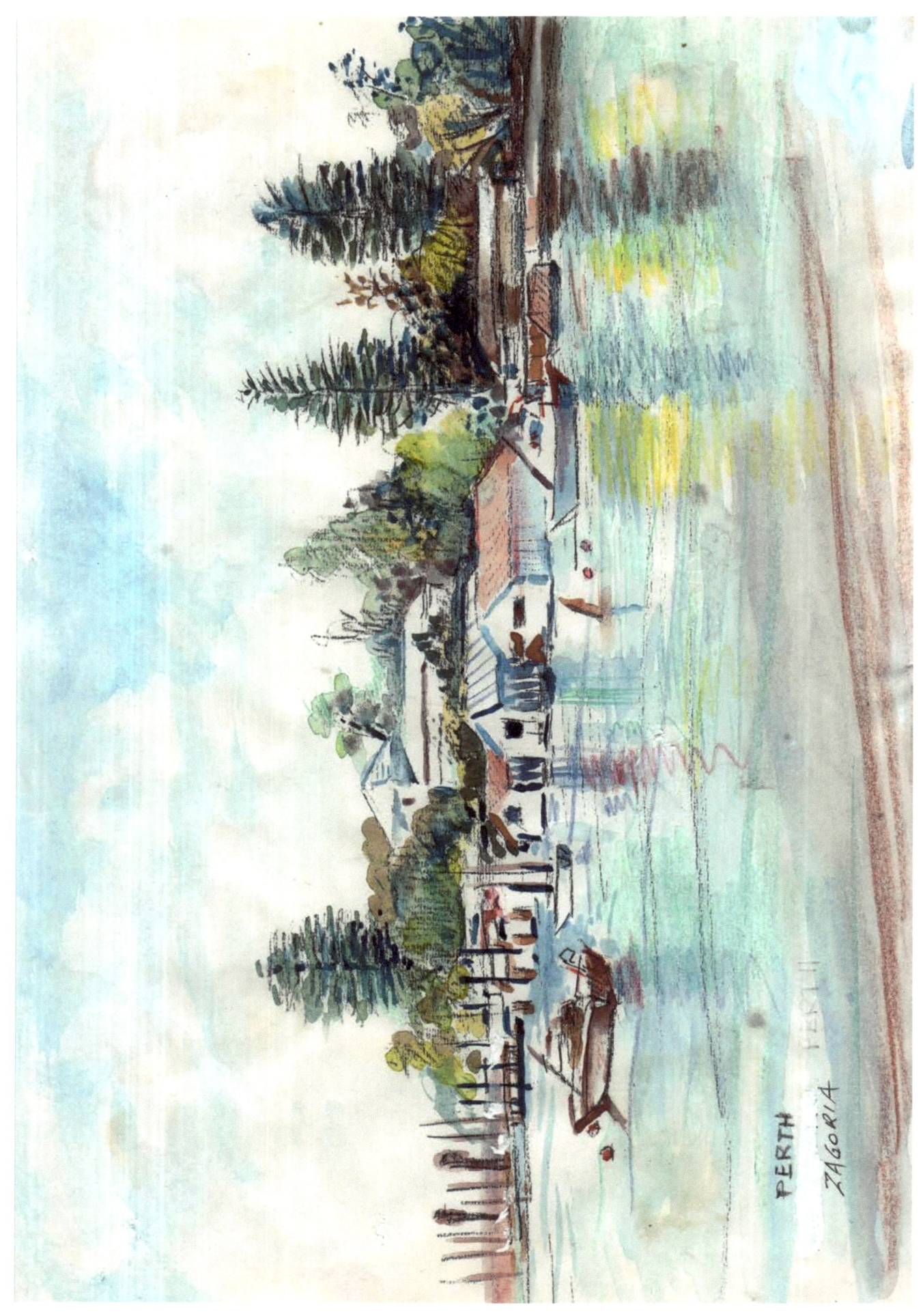

PERTH

ZAGORIA

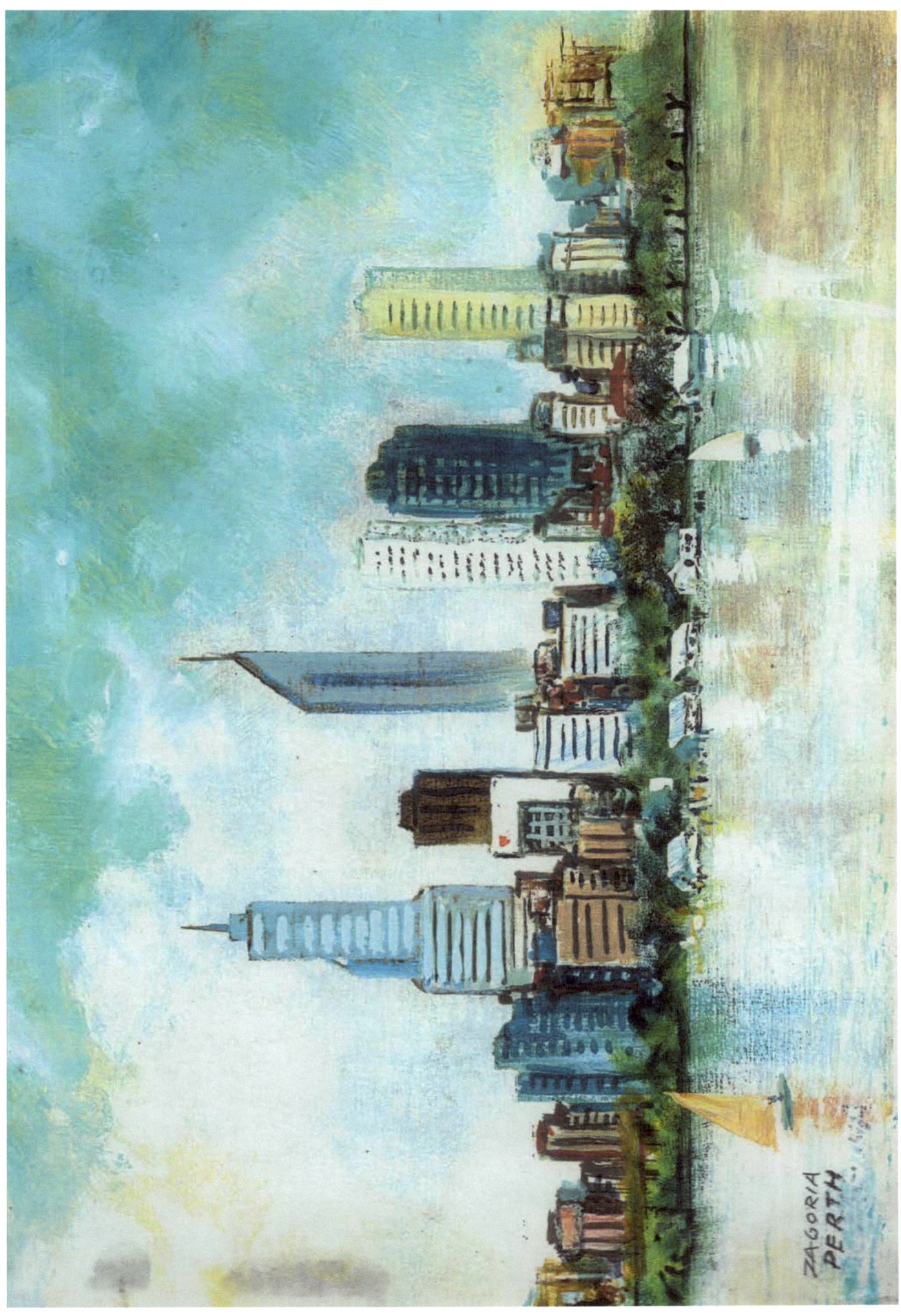

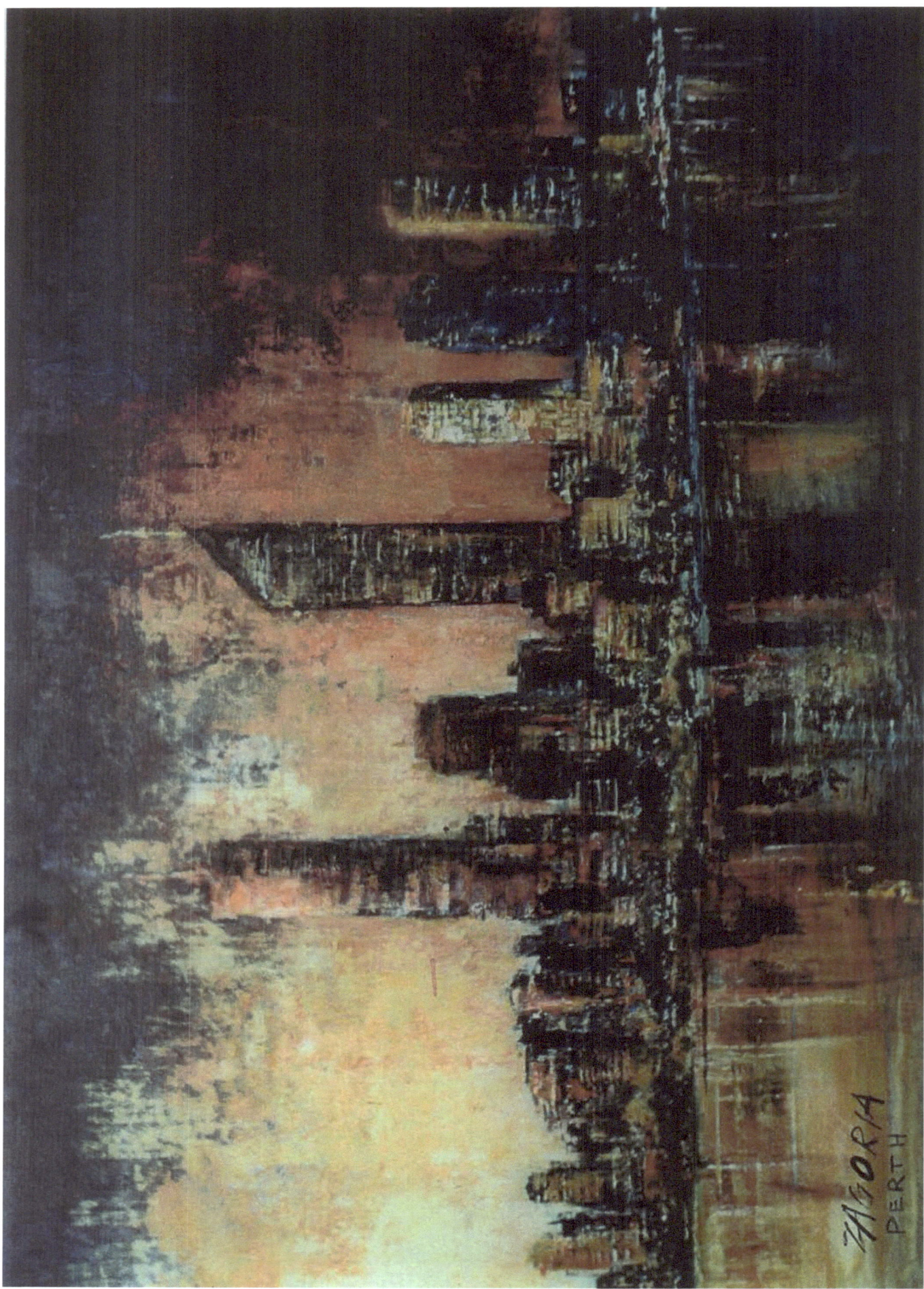

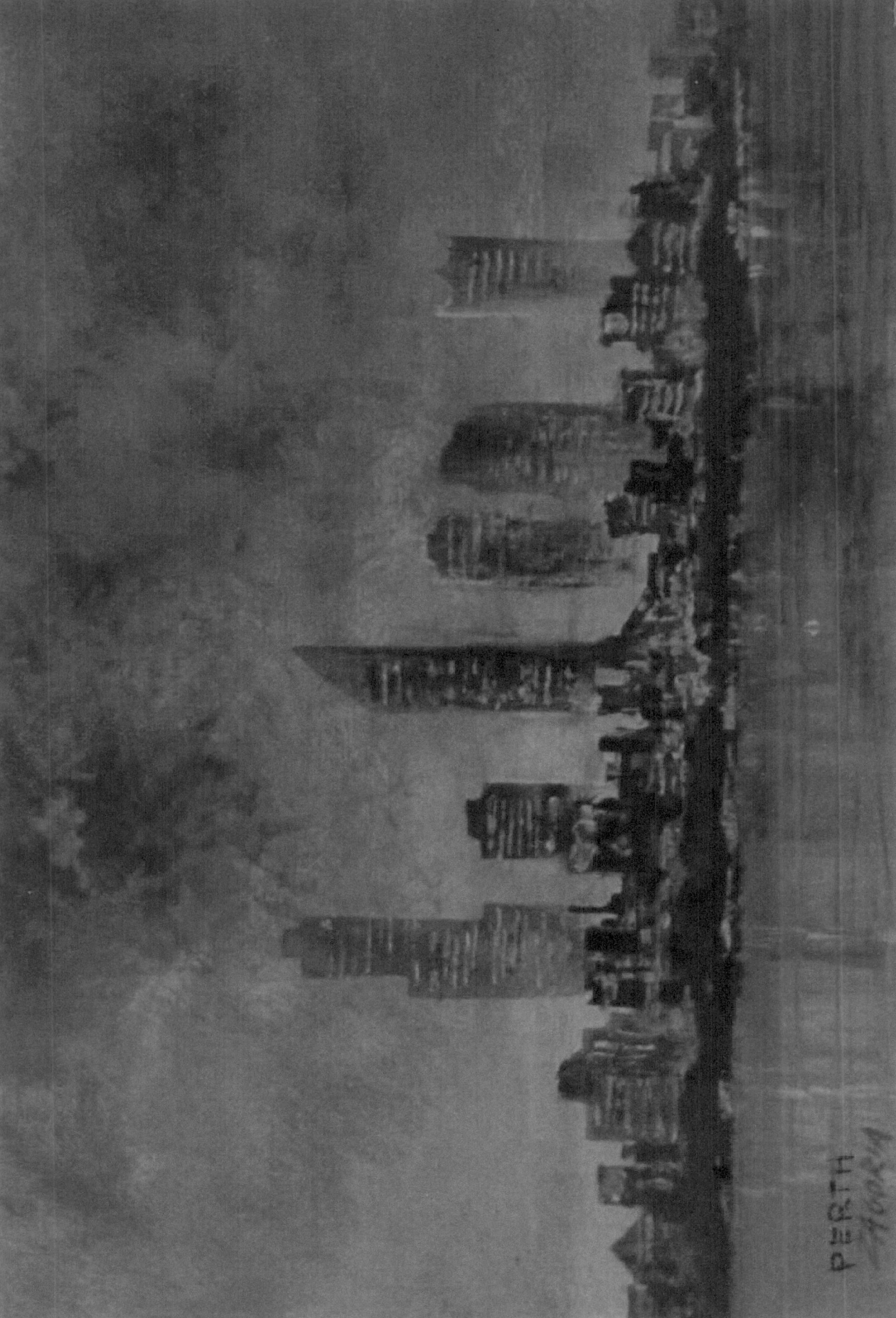

PERTH
HOBART

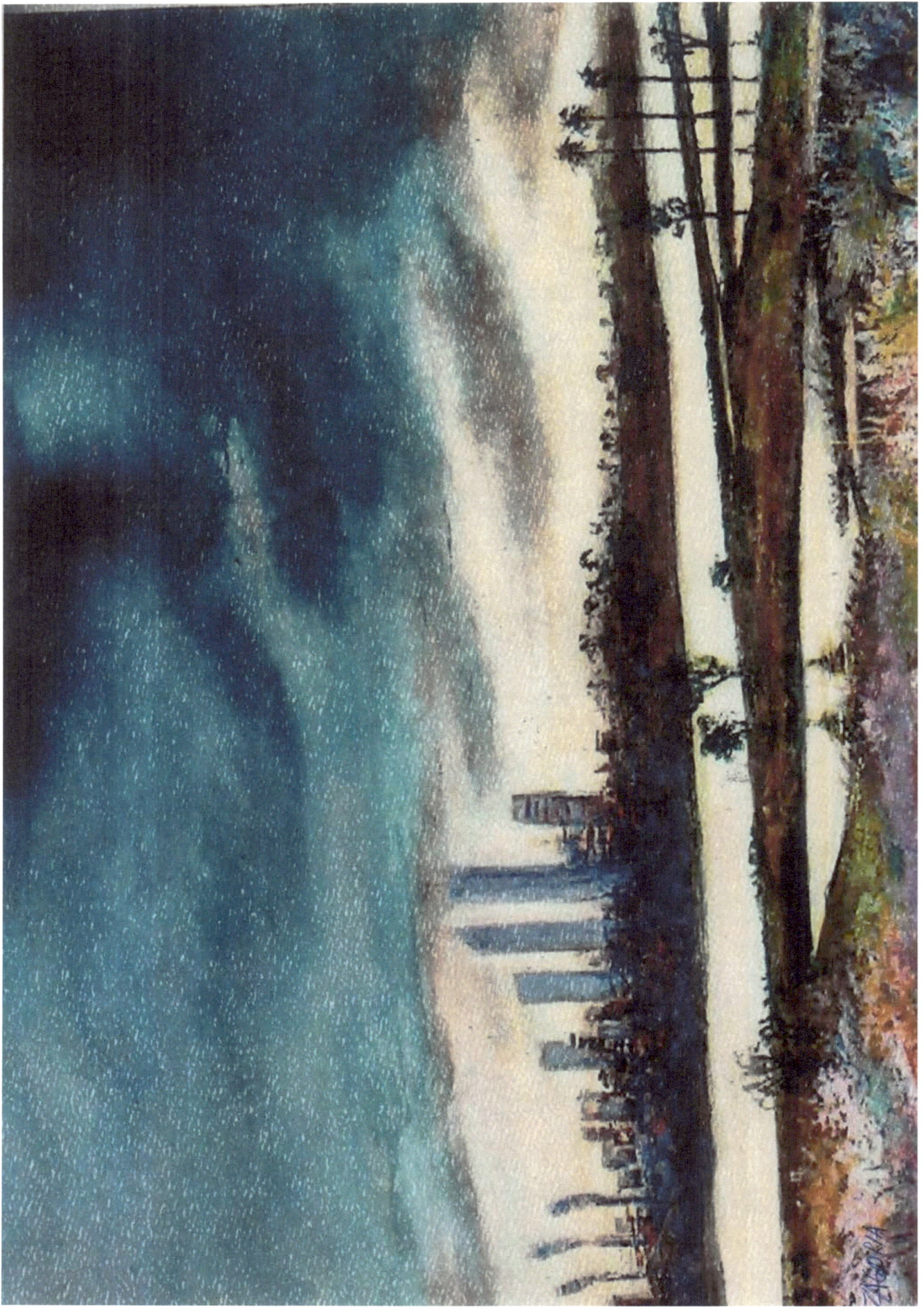

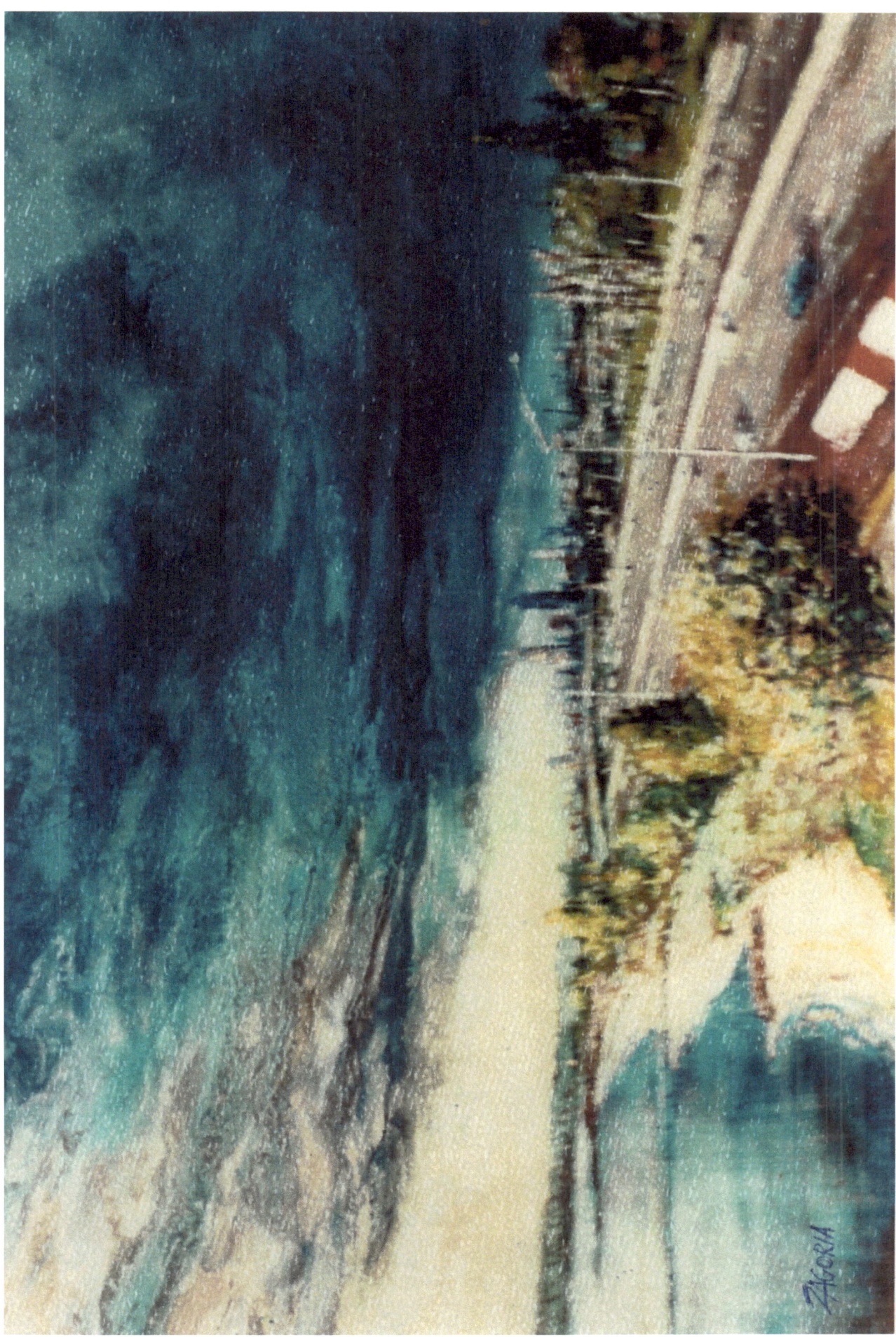

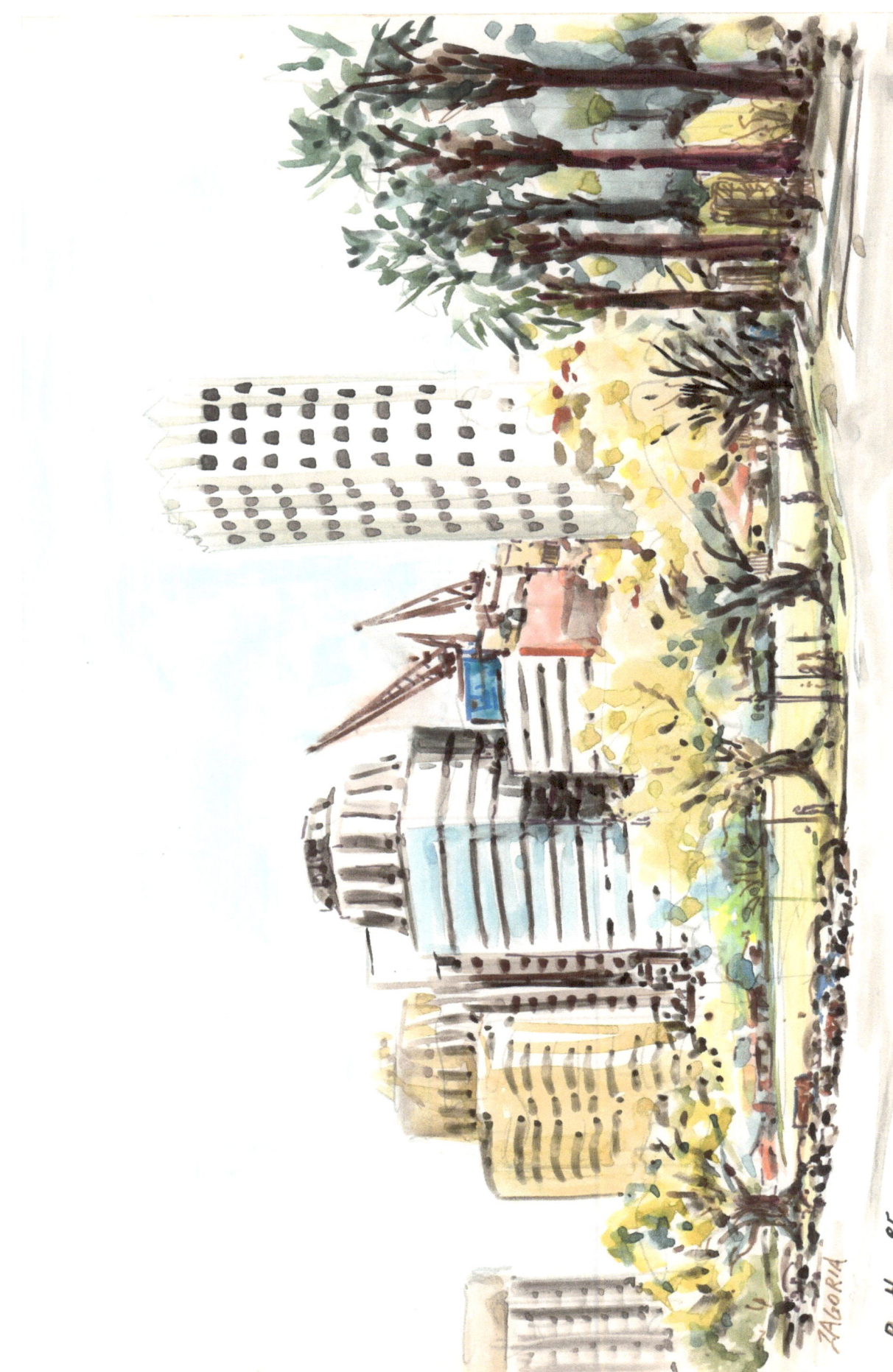

ZABORIA

Perth in 85

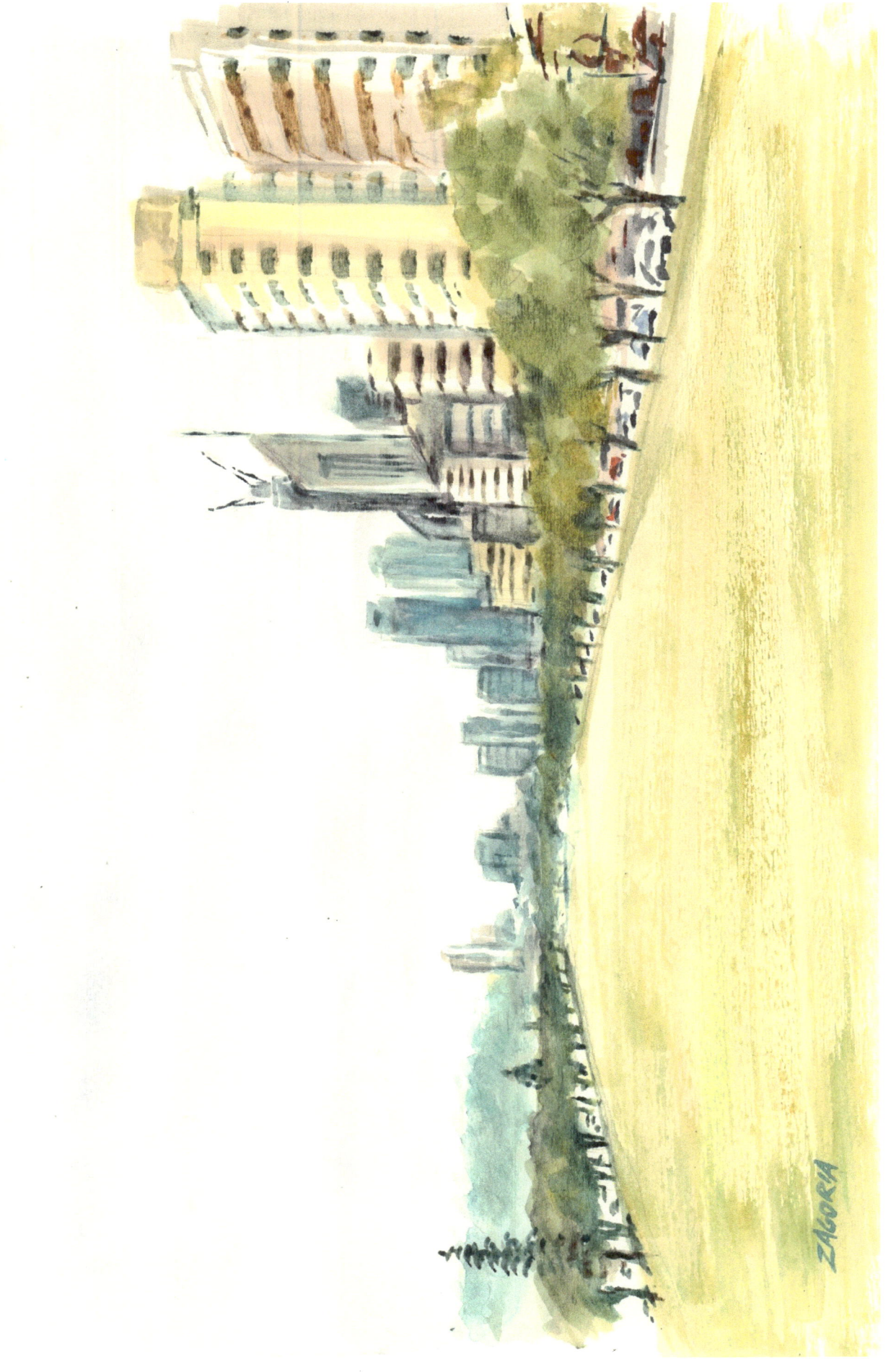

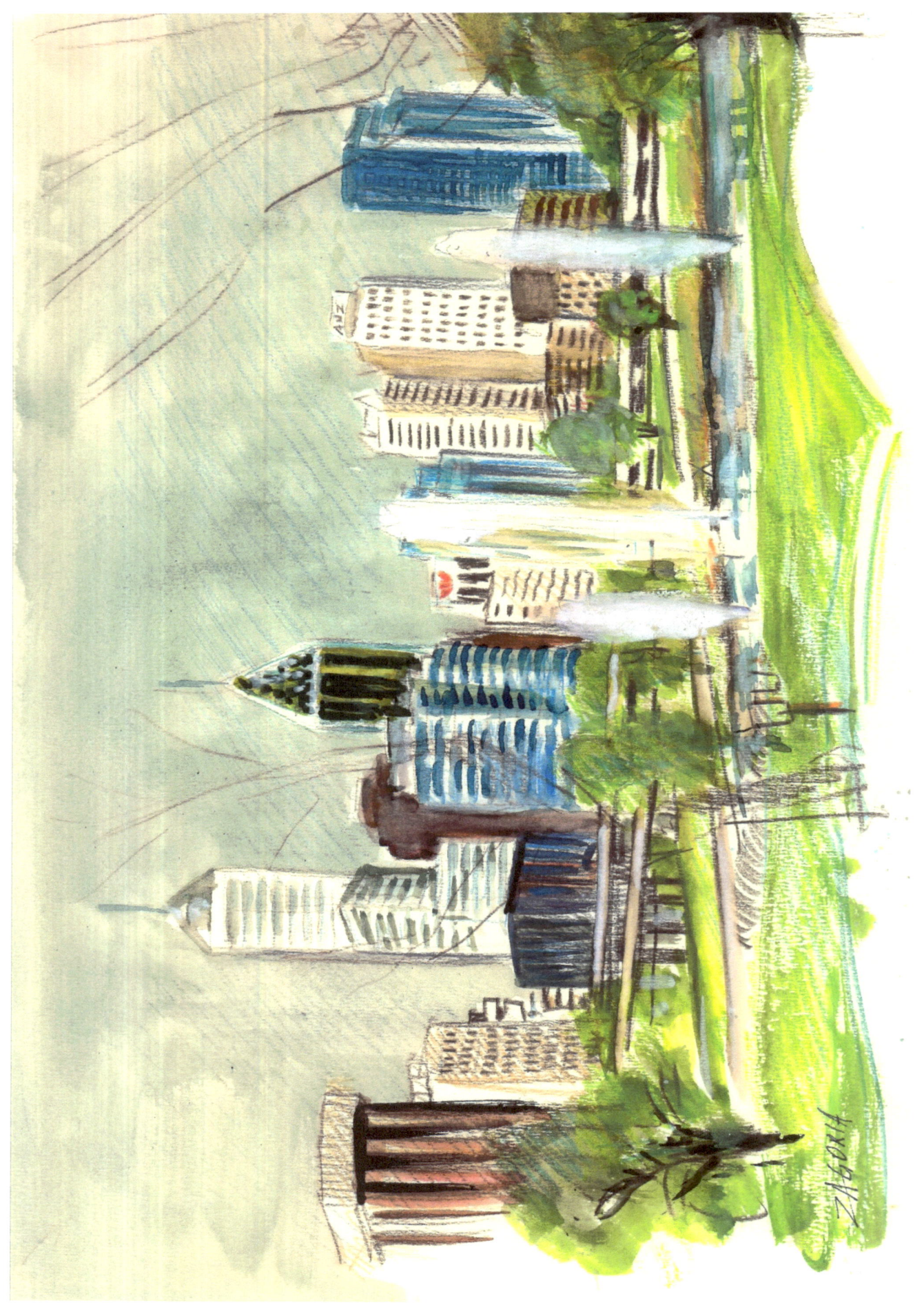

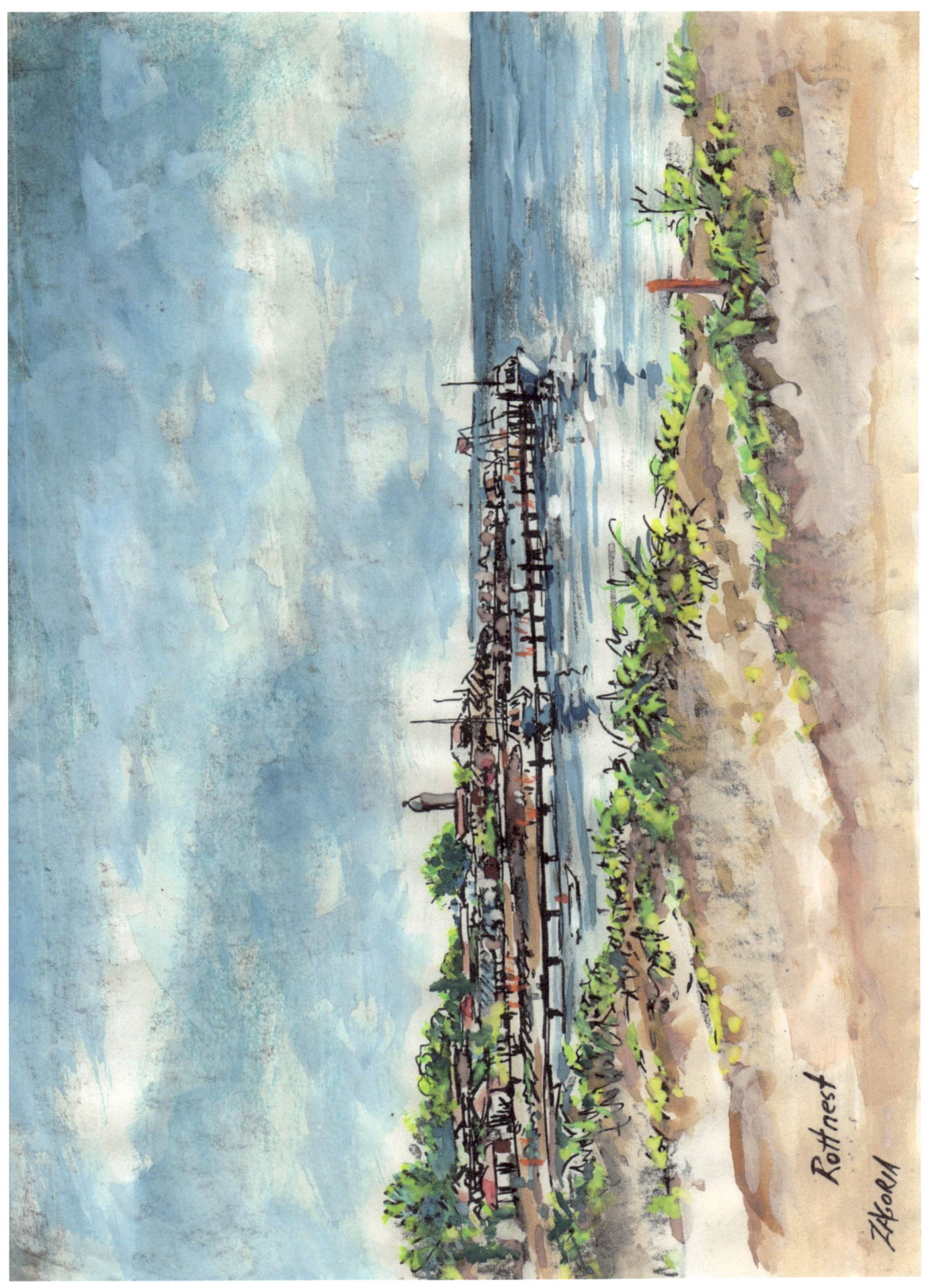

Rottnest

ZAGORA

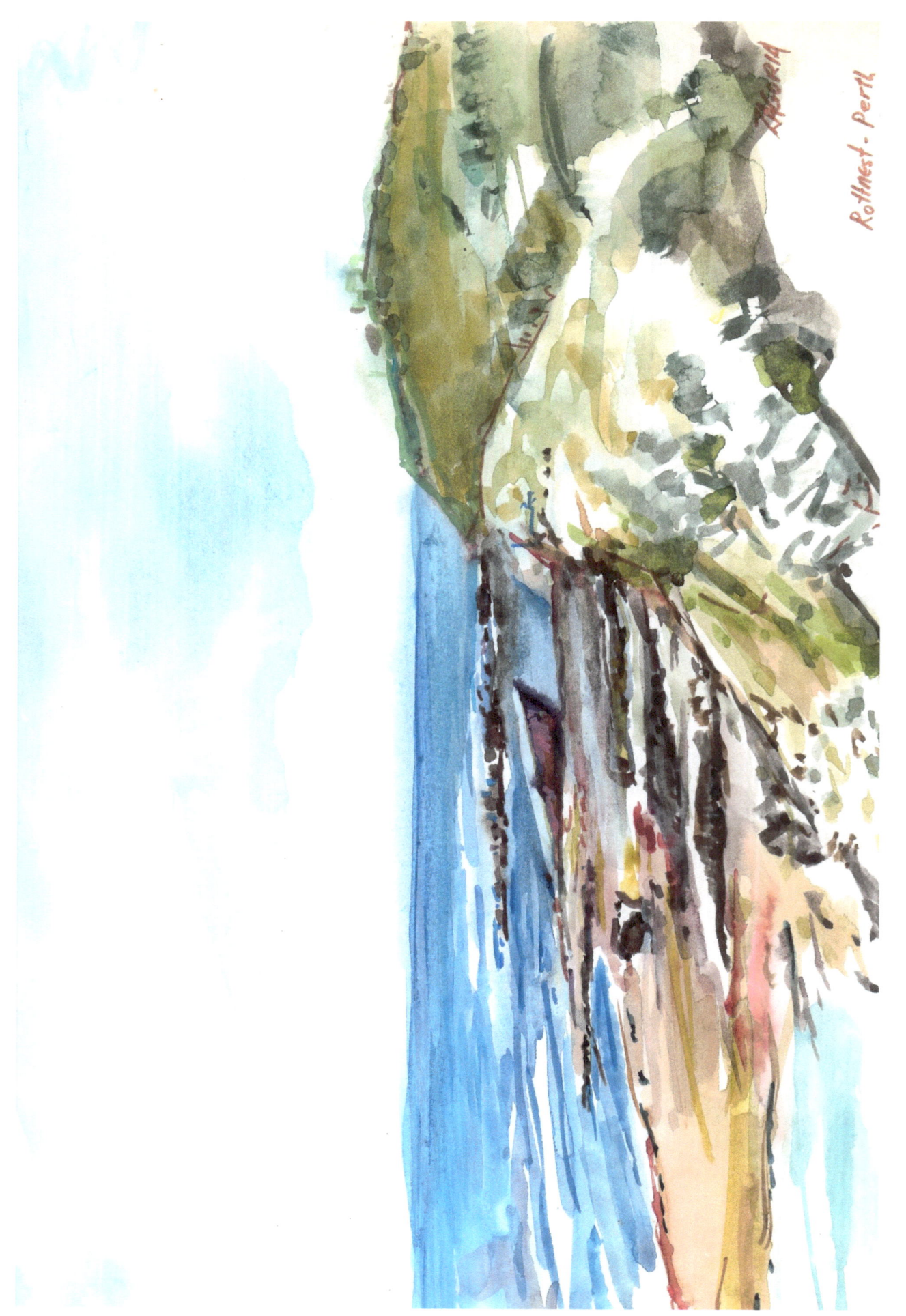

ARBORIA

Rottnest - Perth

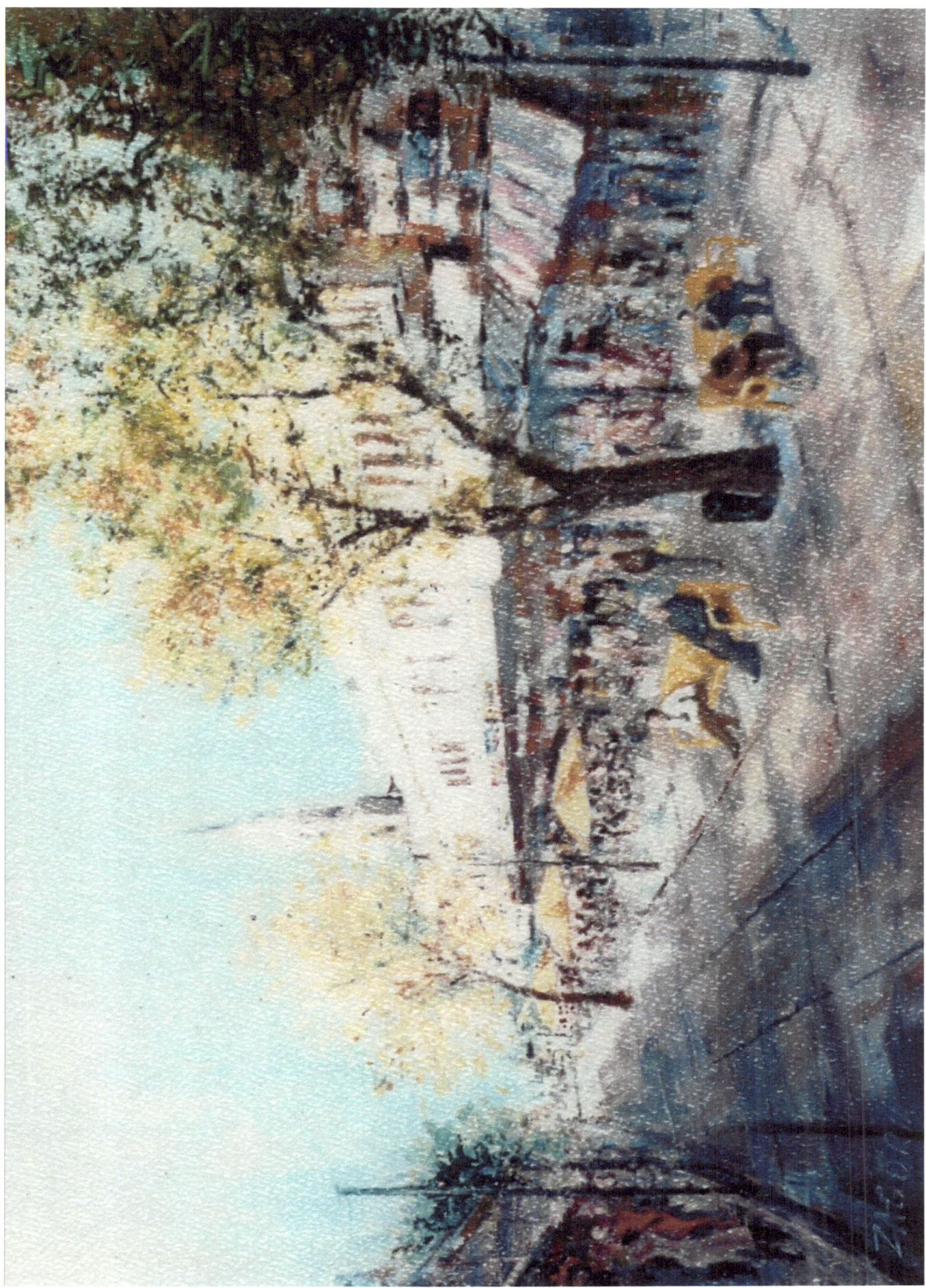

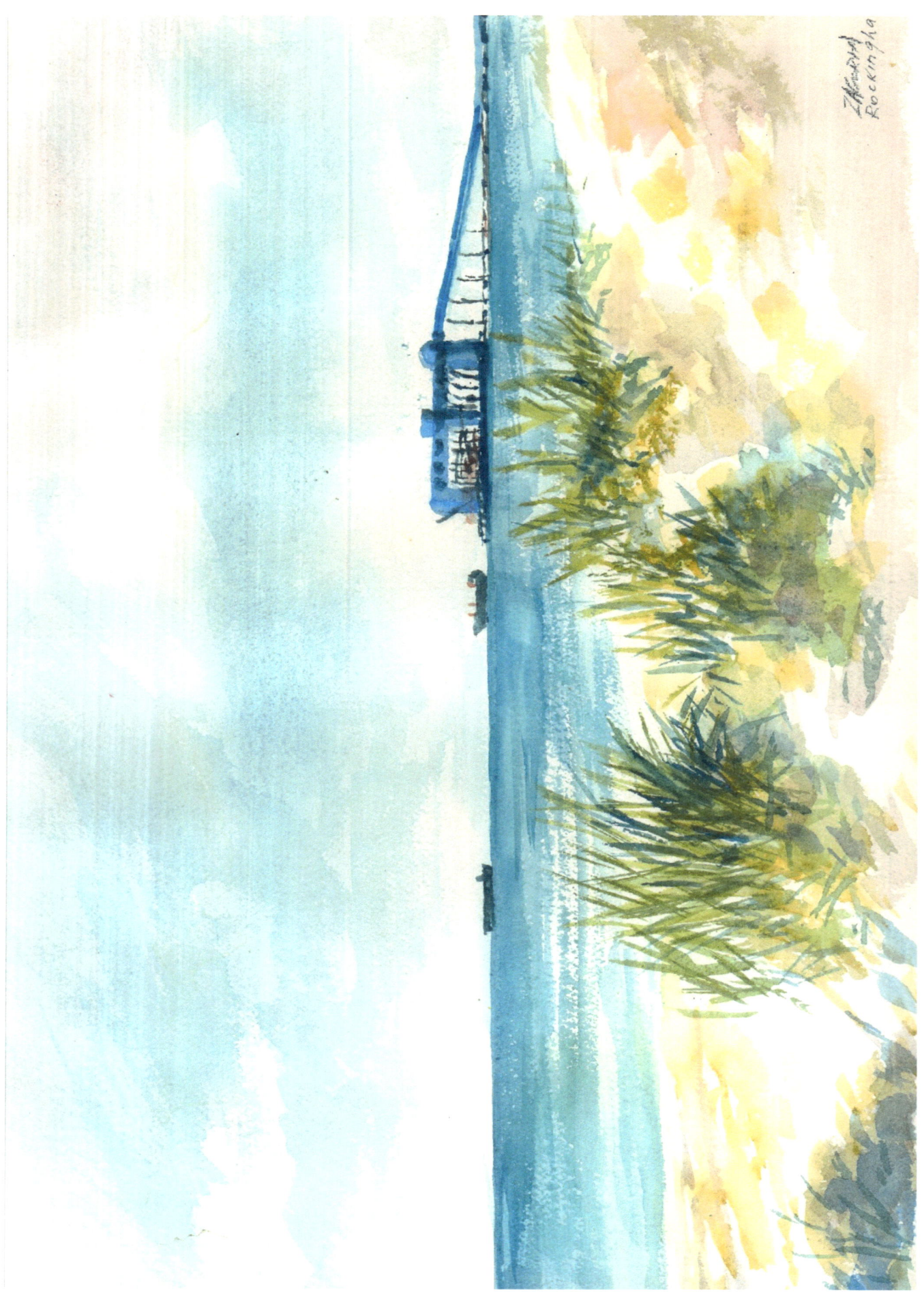

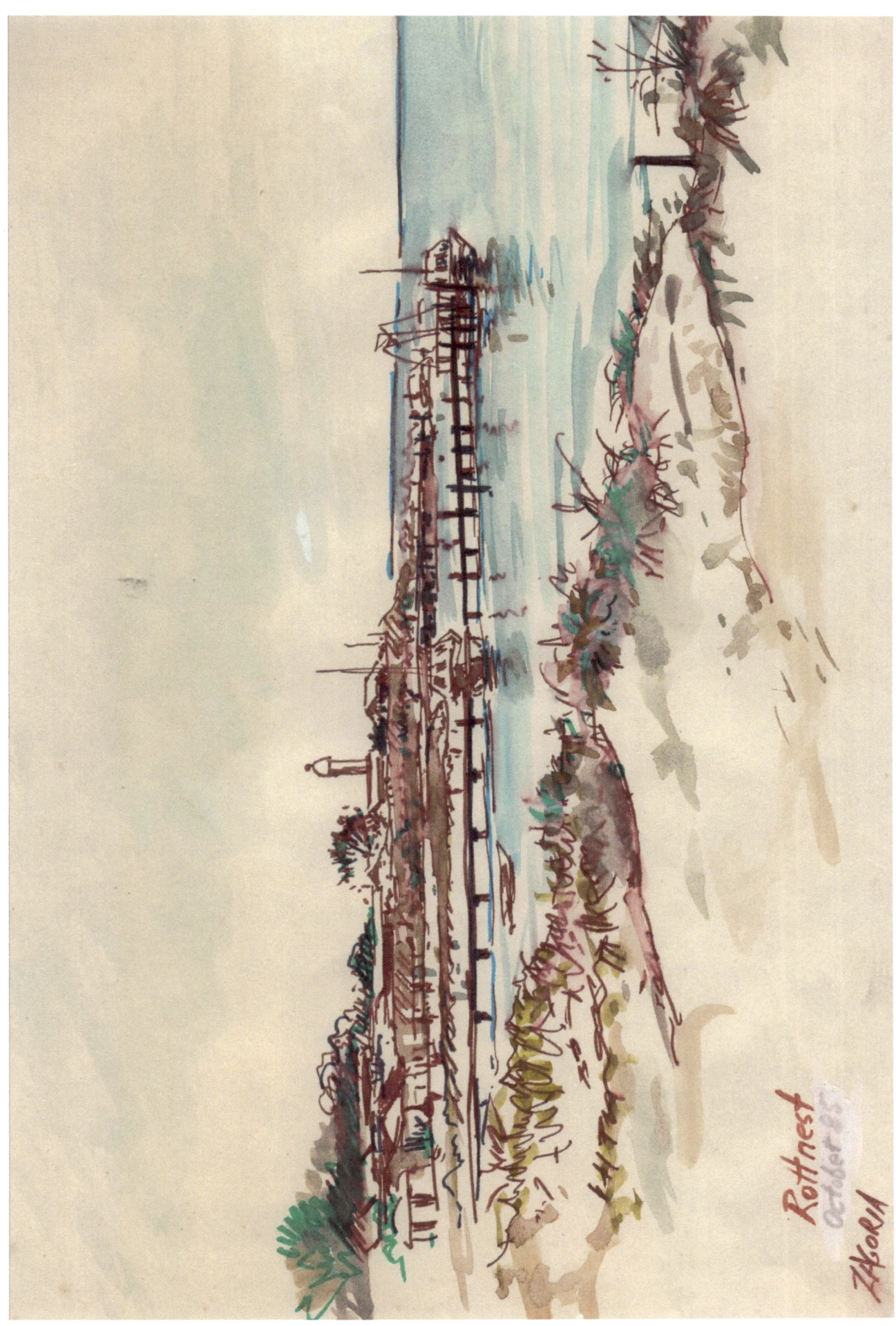

Rottnest
October 85

ZAGORIA

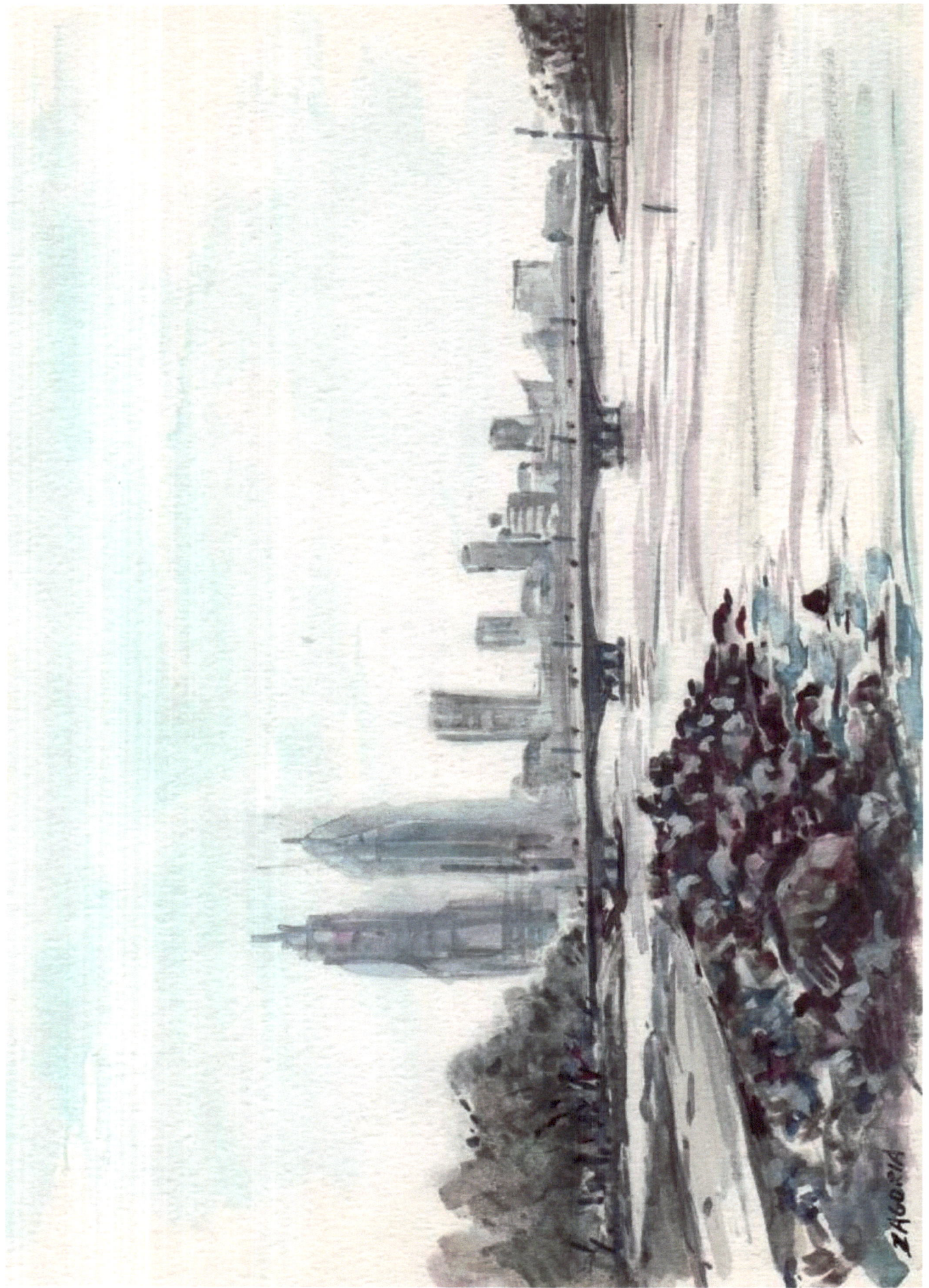

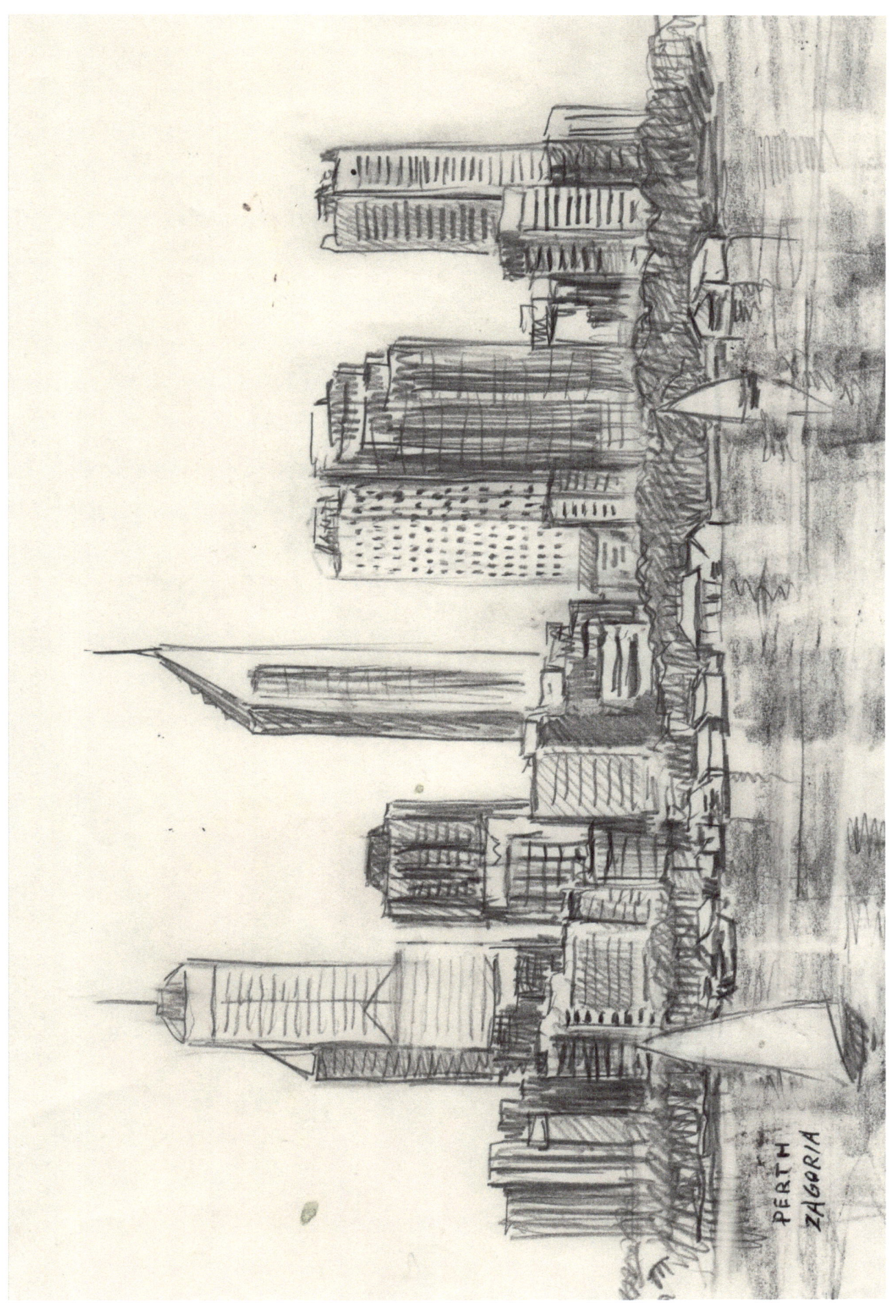

PERTH
ZAGORIA

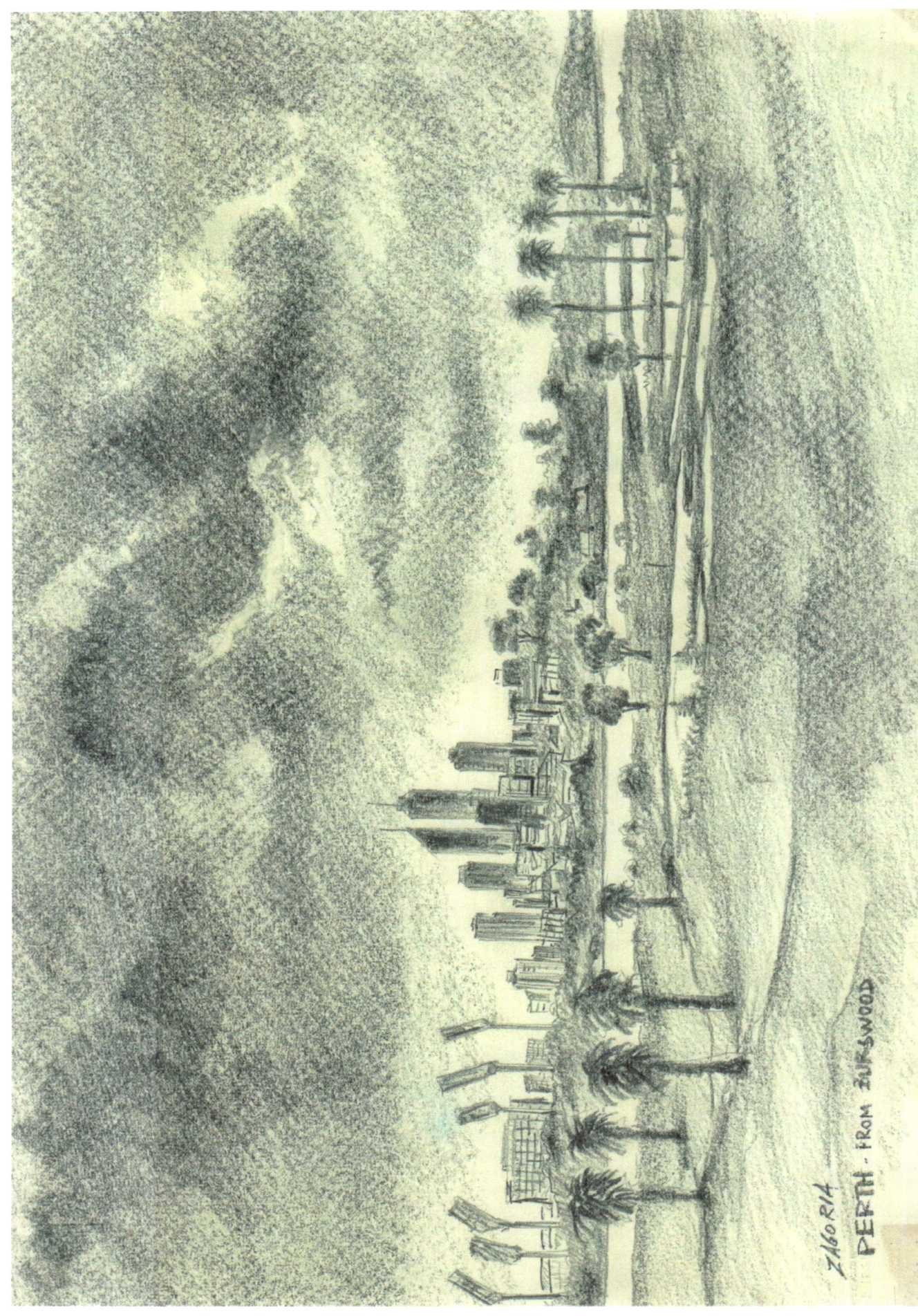

ZAGORIA

PERTH - FROM BURSWOOD

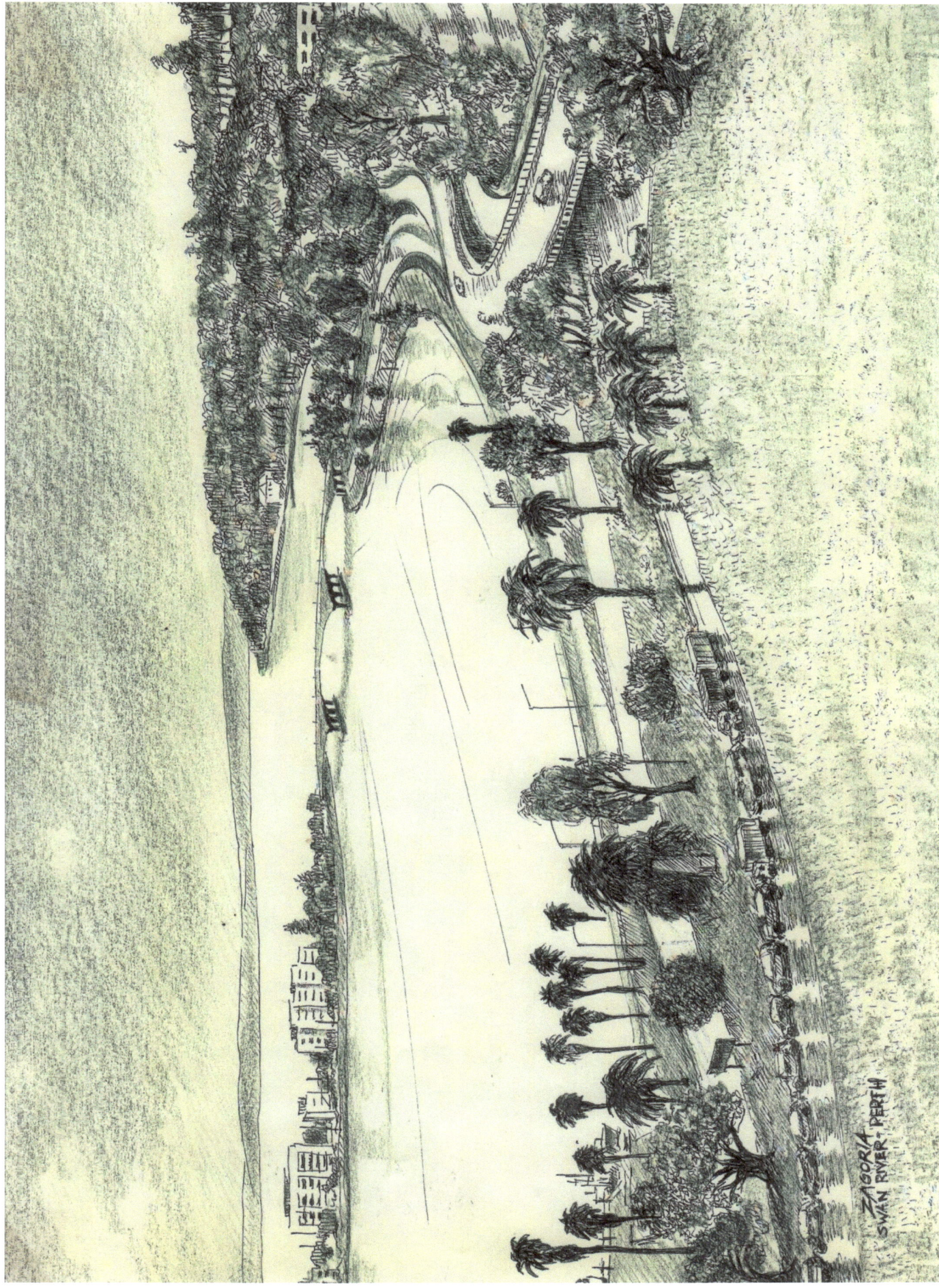

ZAGORIA
SWAN RIVER • PERTH

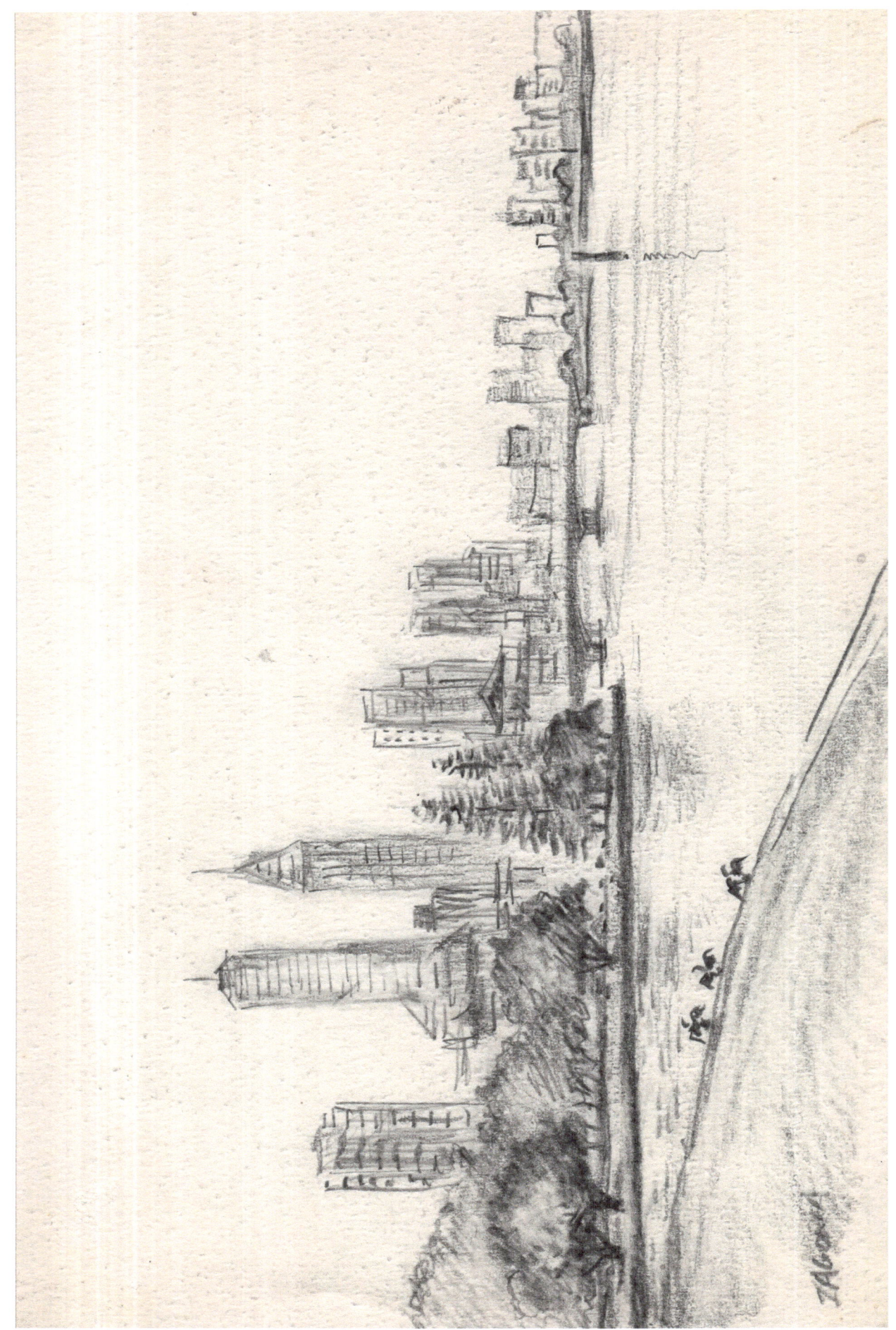

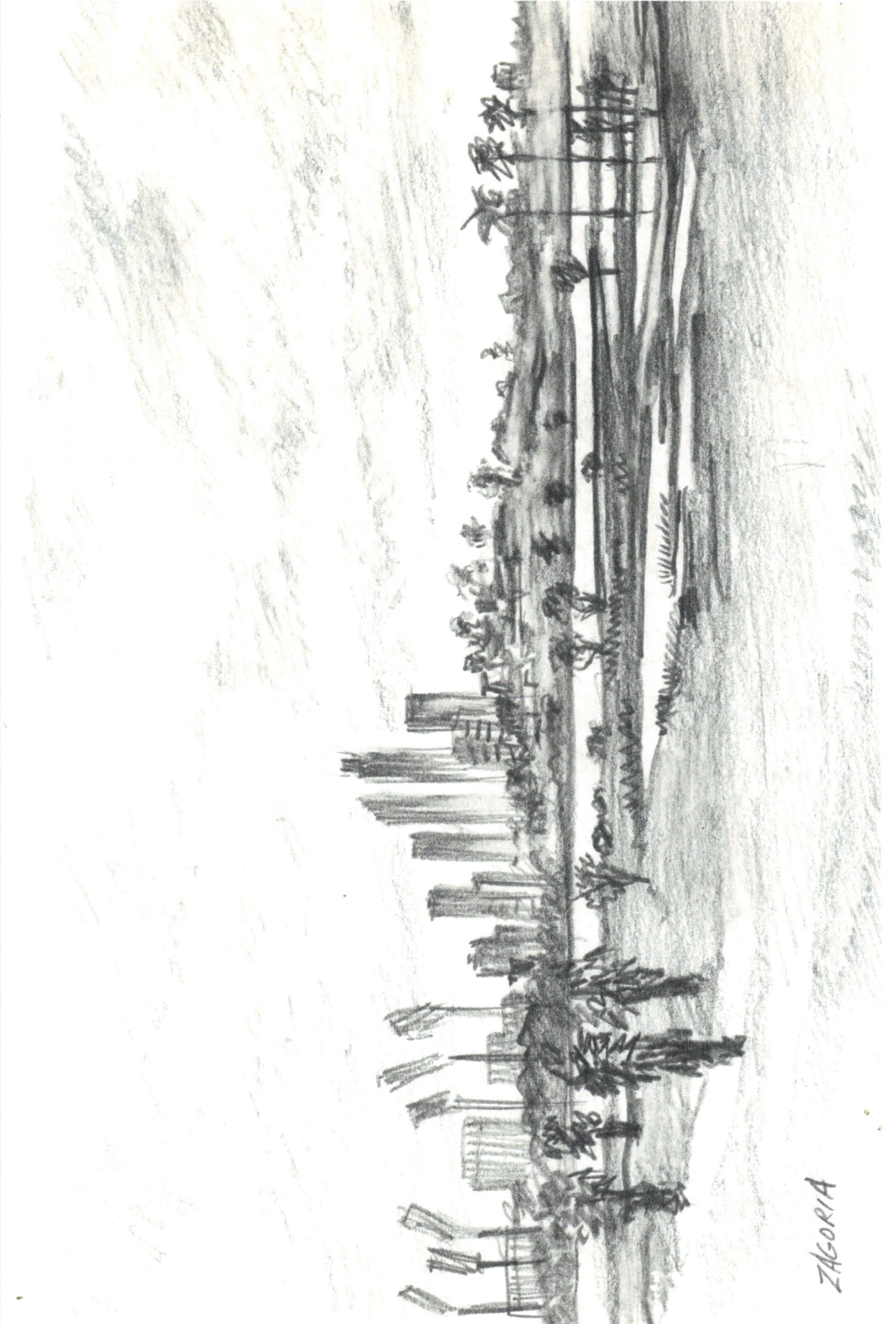

ZAGORIA

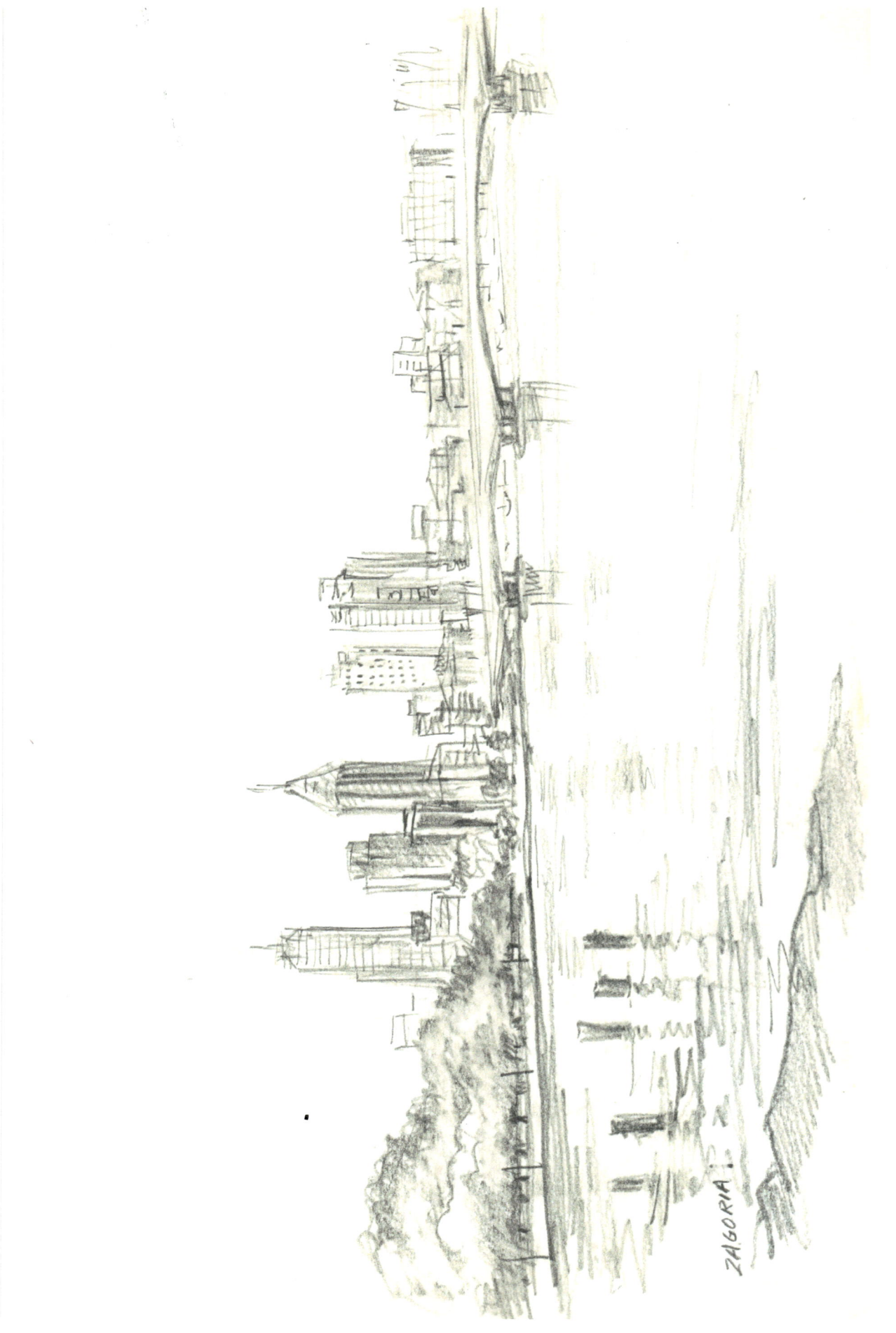

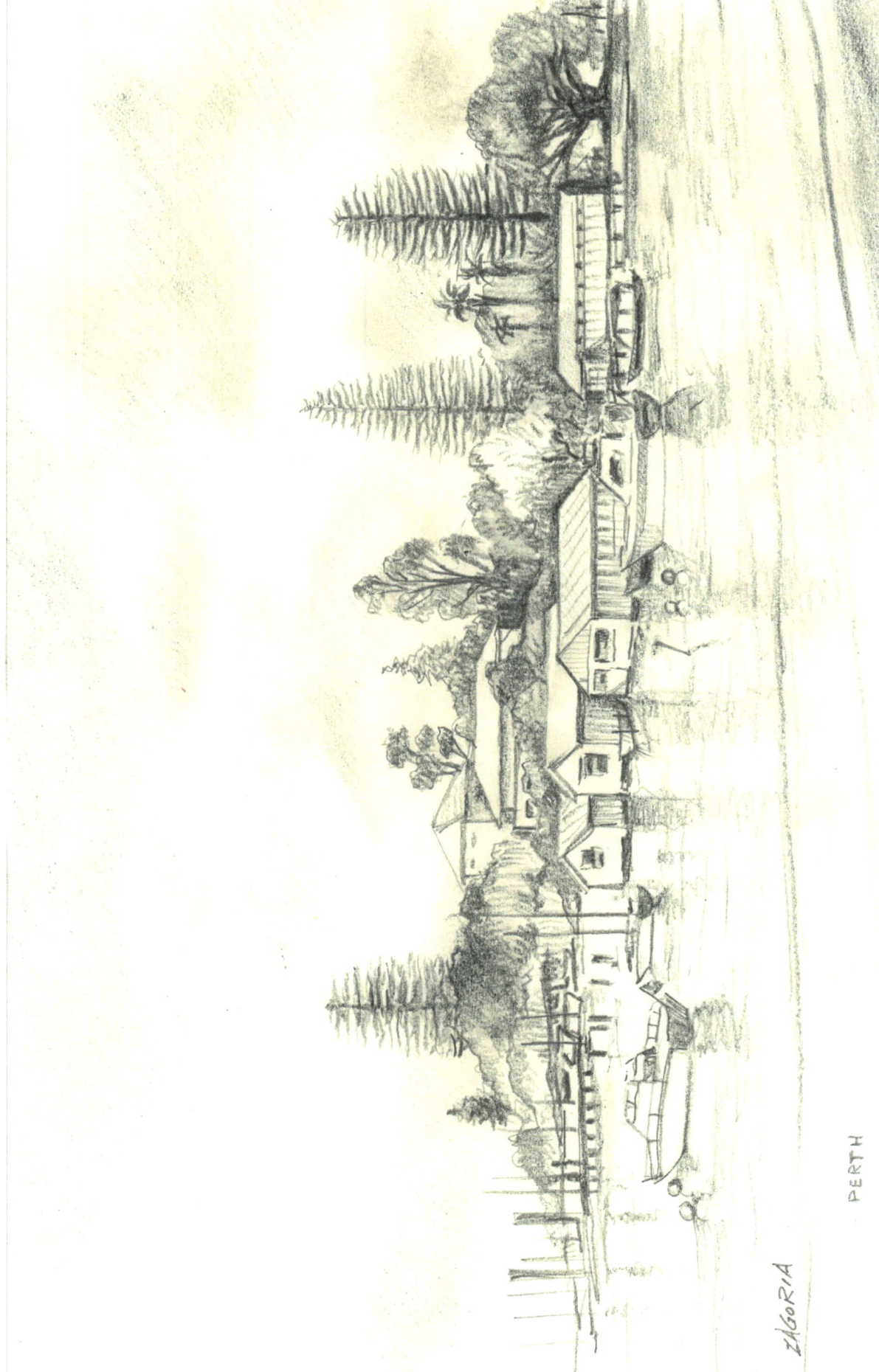

ZAGORIA

PERTH

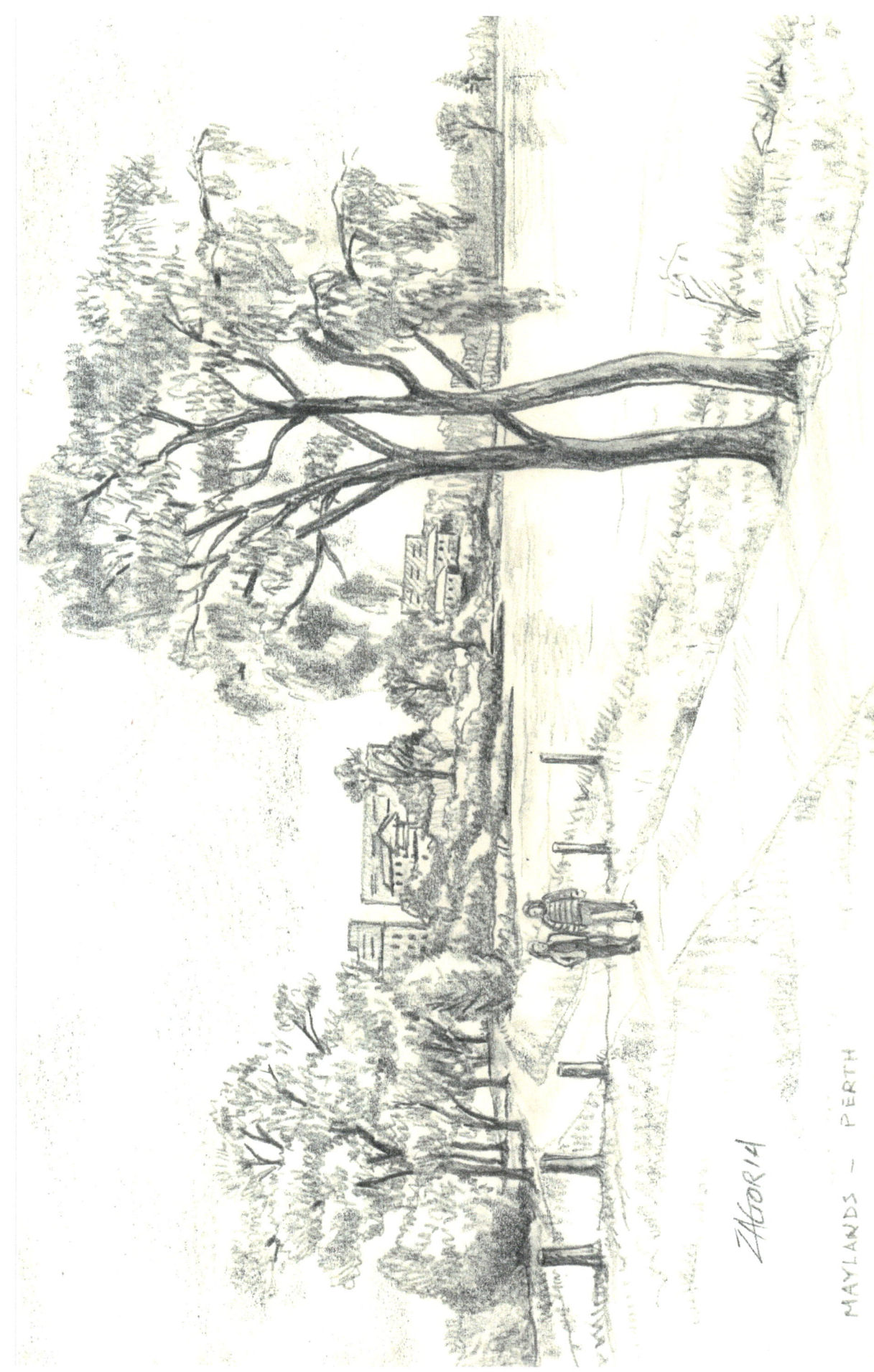

ZAGOR14

MAYLANDS — PERTH

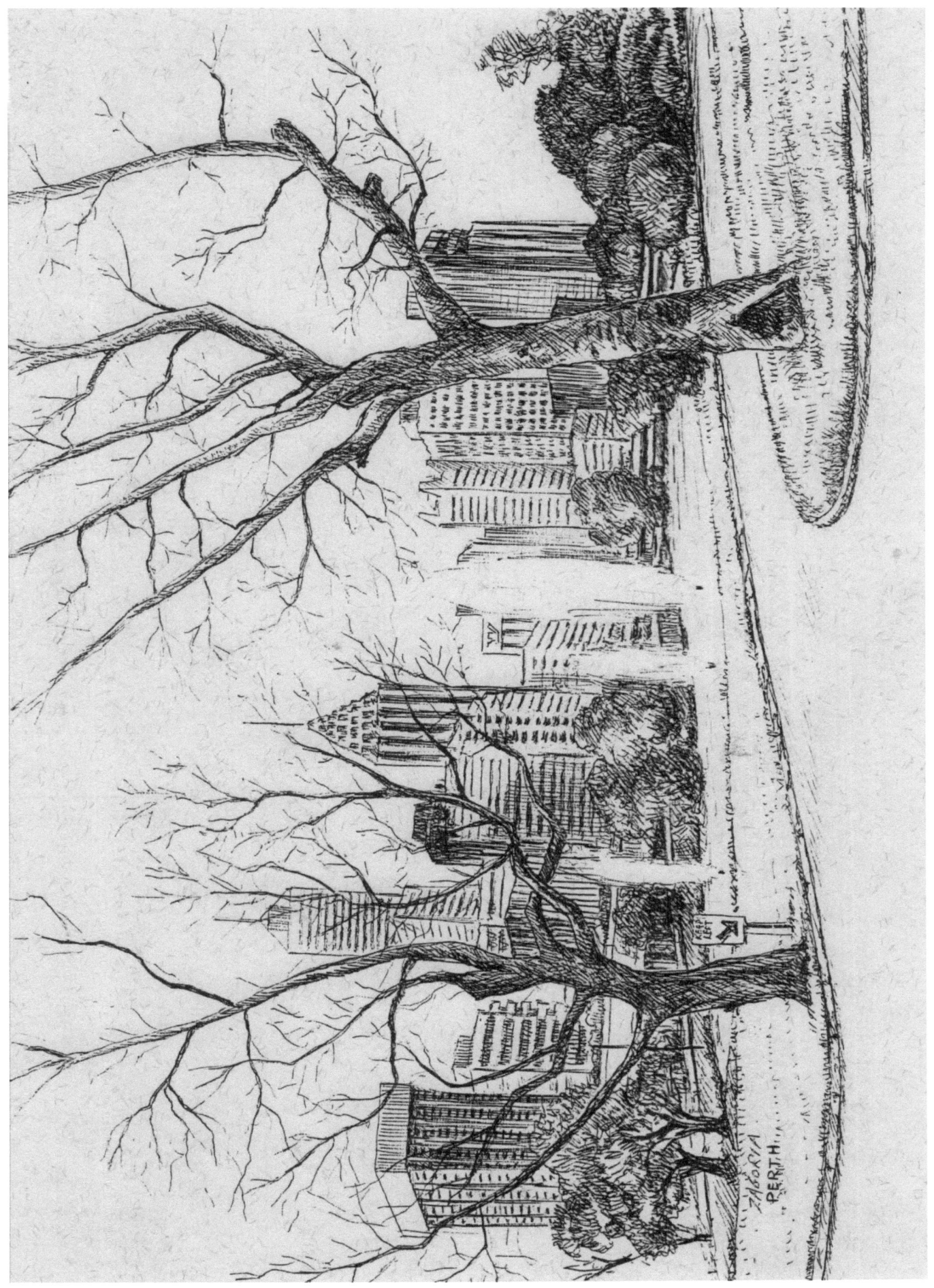

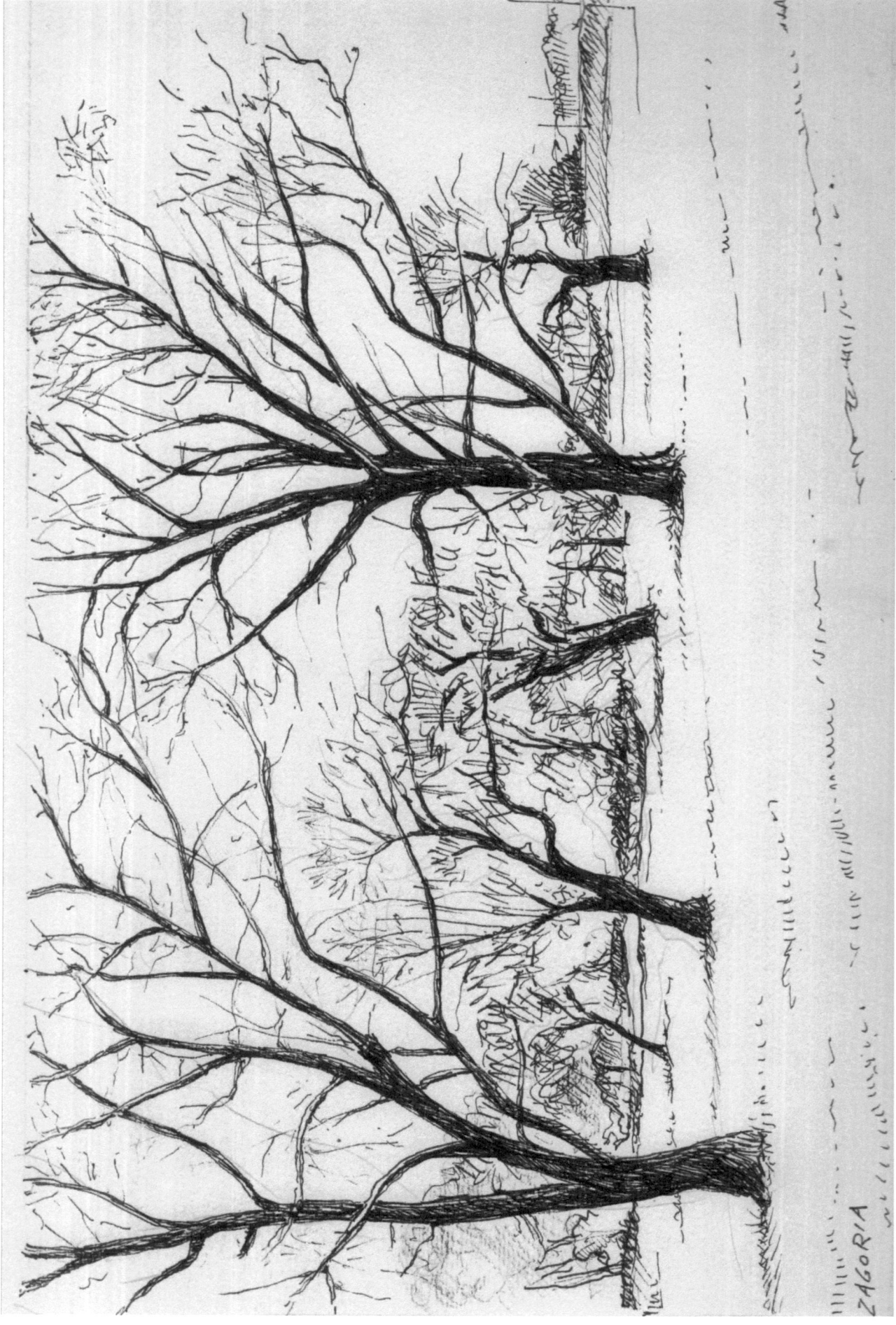

ZAGORIA

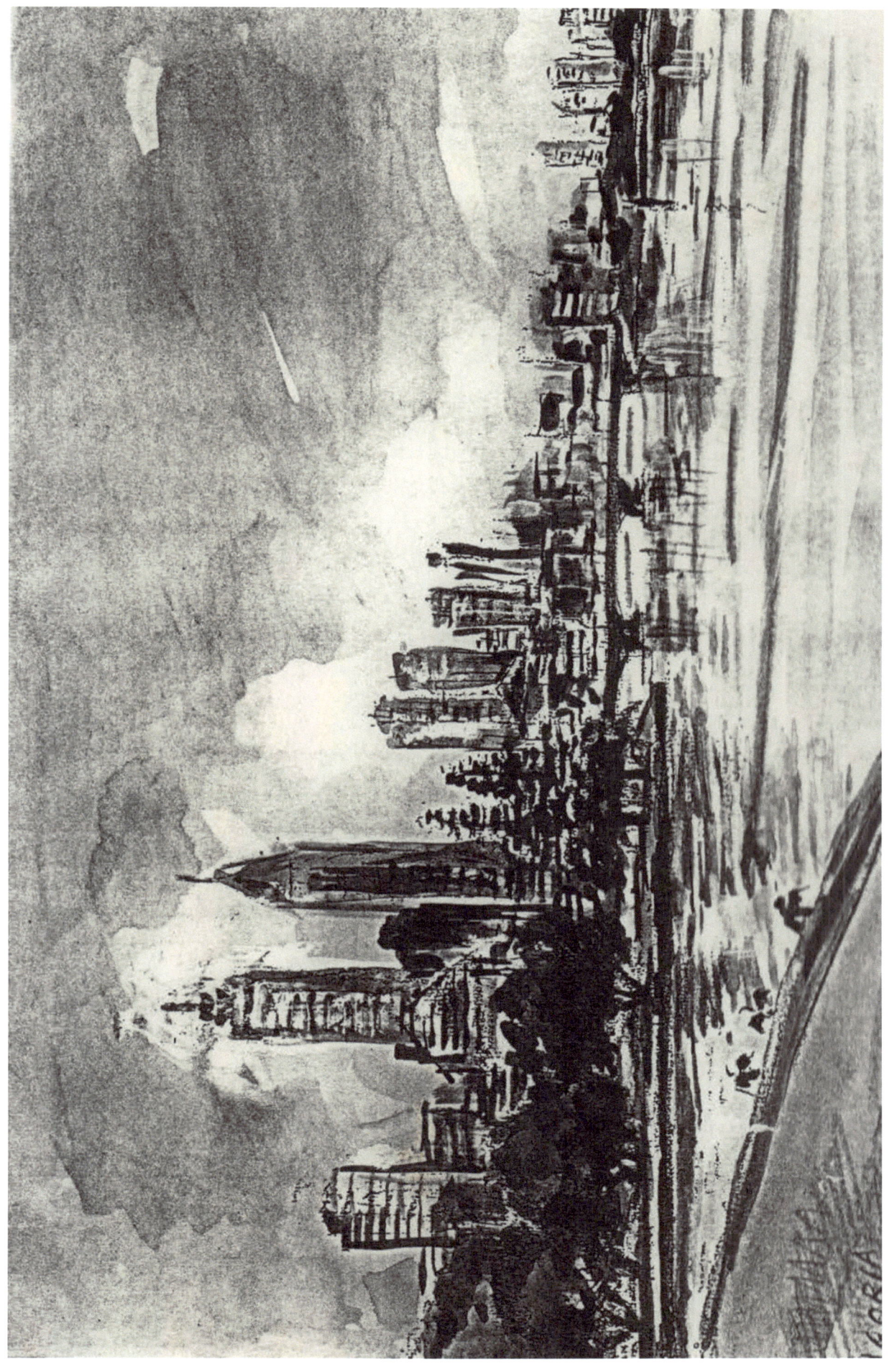

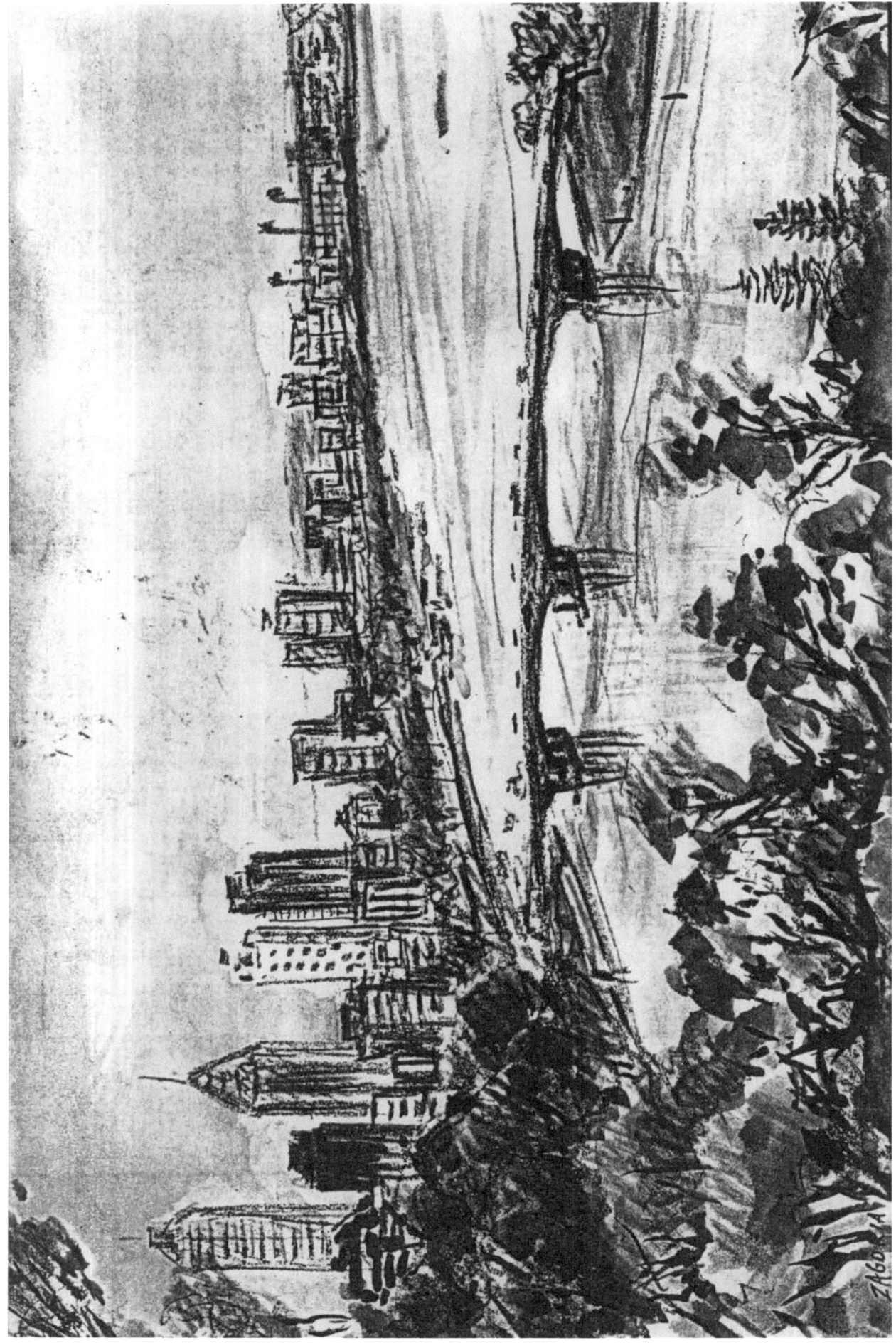

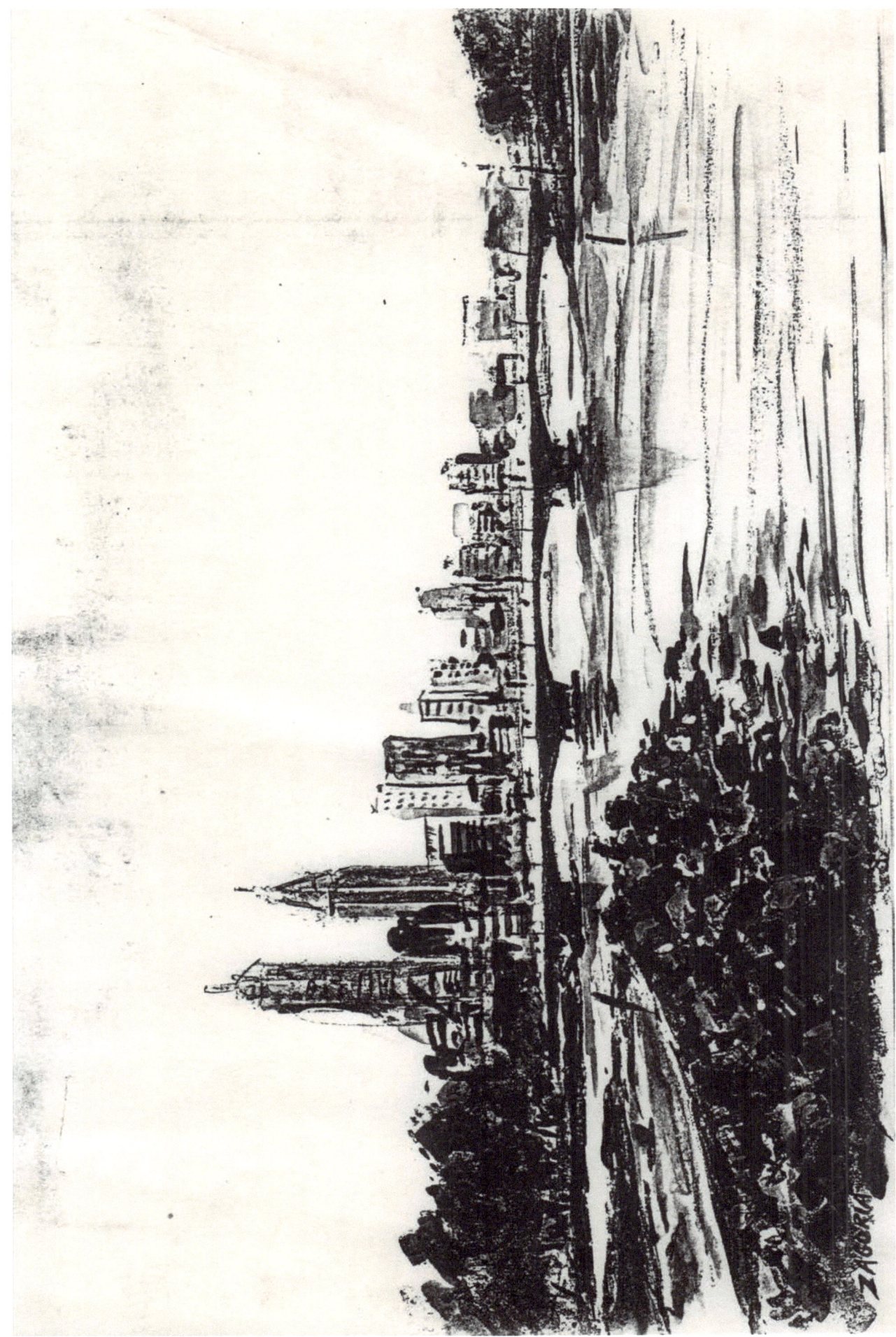

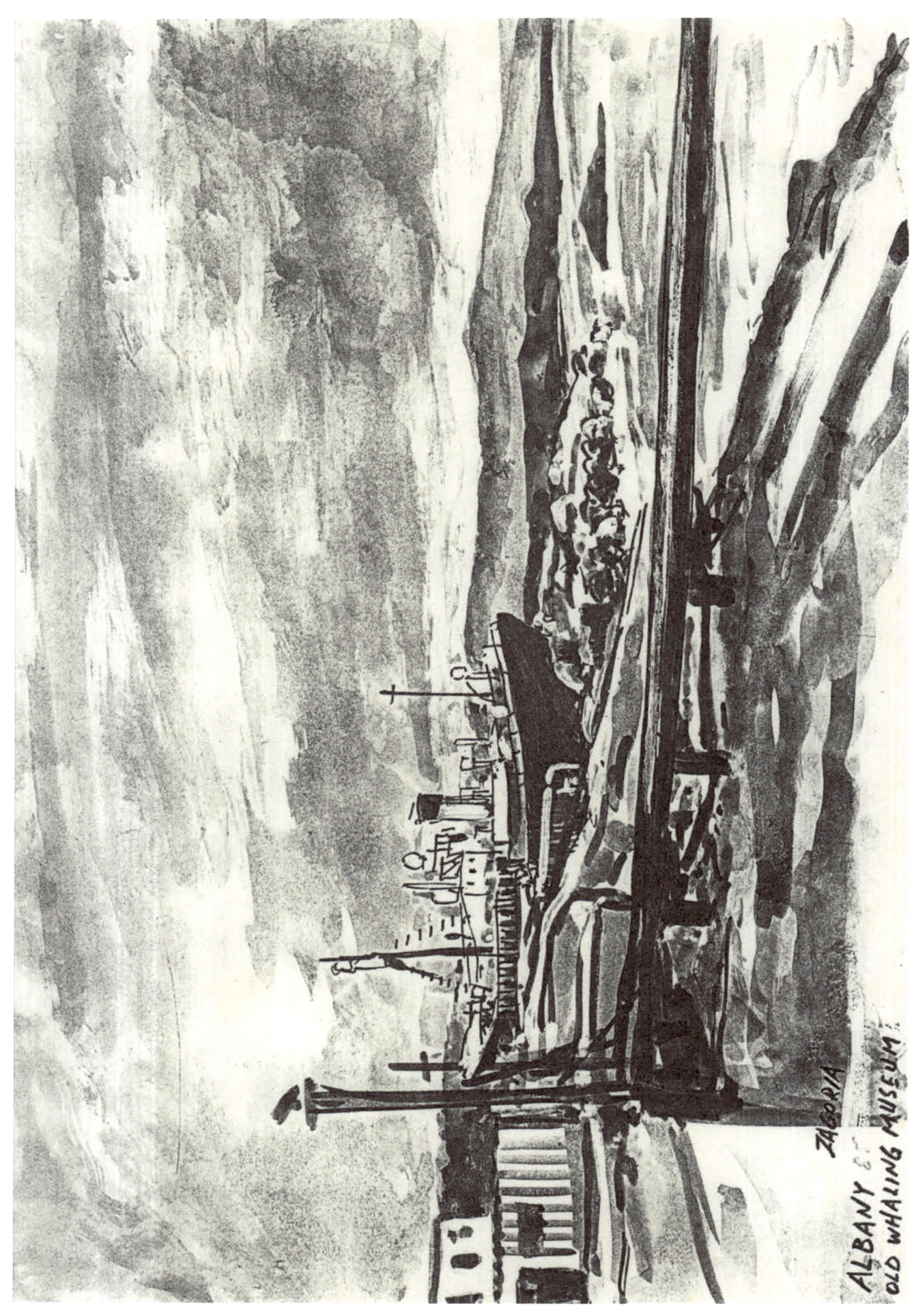

ZAGORIA

ALBANY &
OLD WHALING MUSEUM :

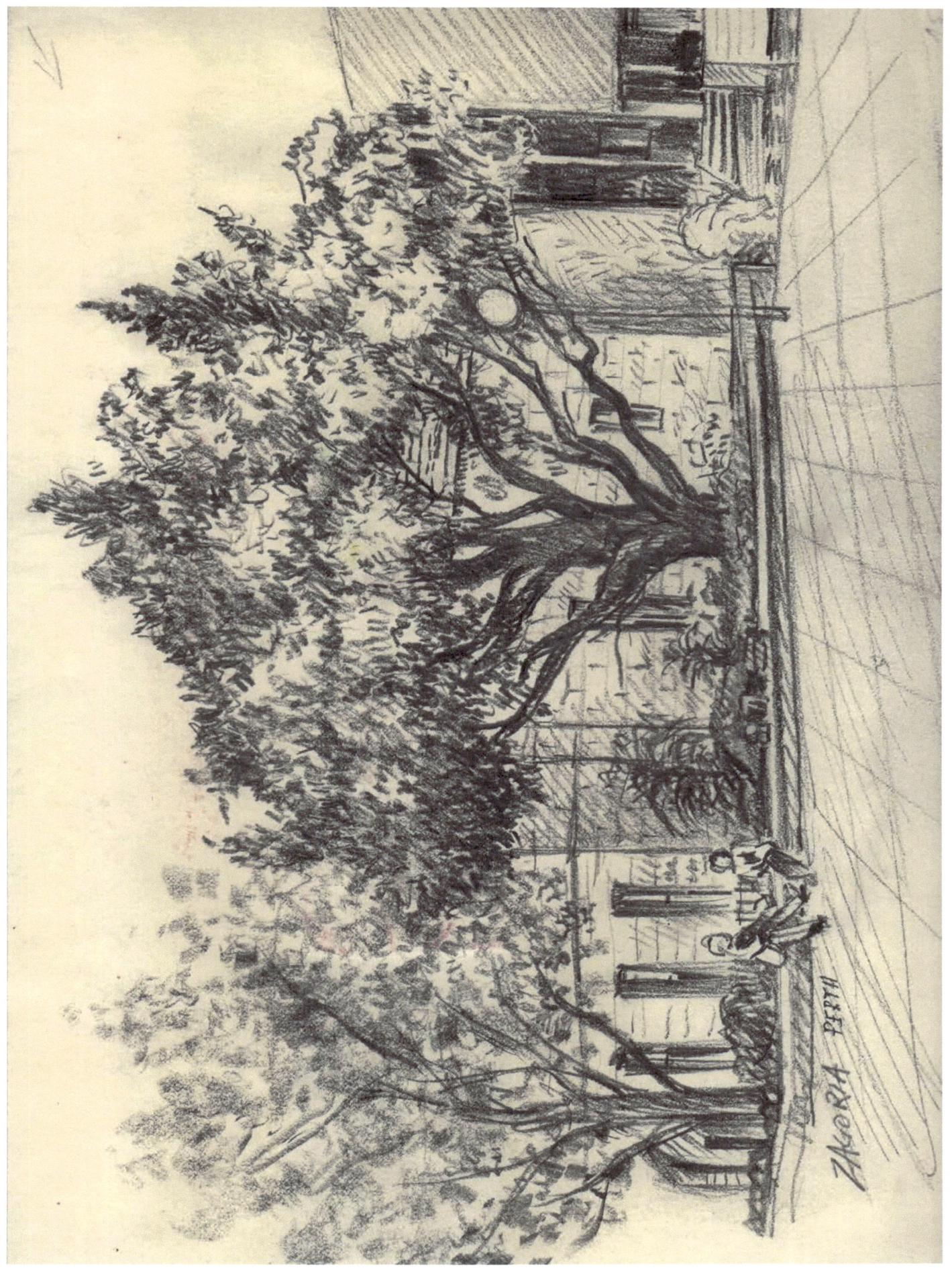

ZAGORIA PERTH

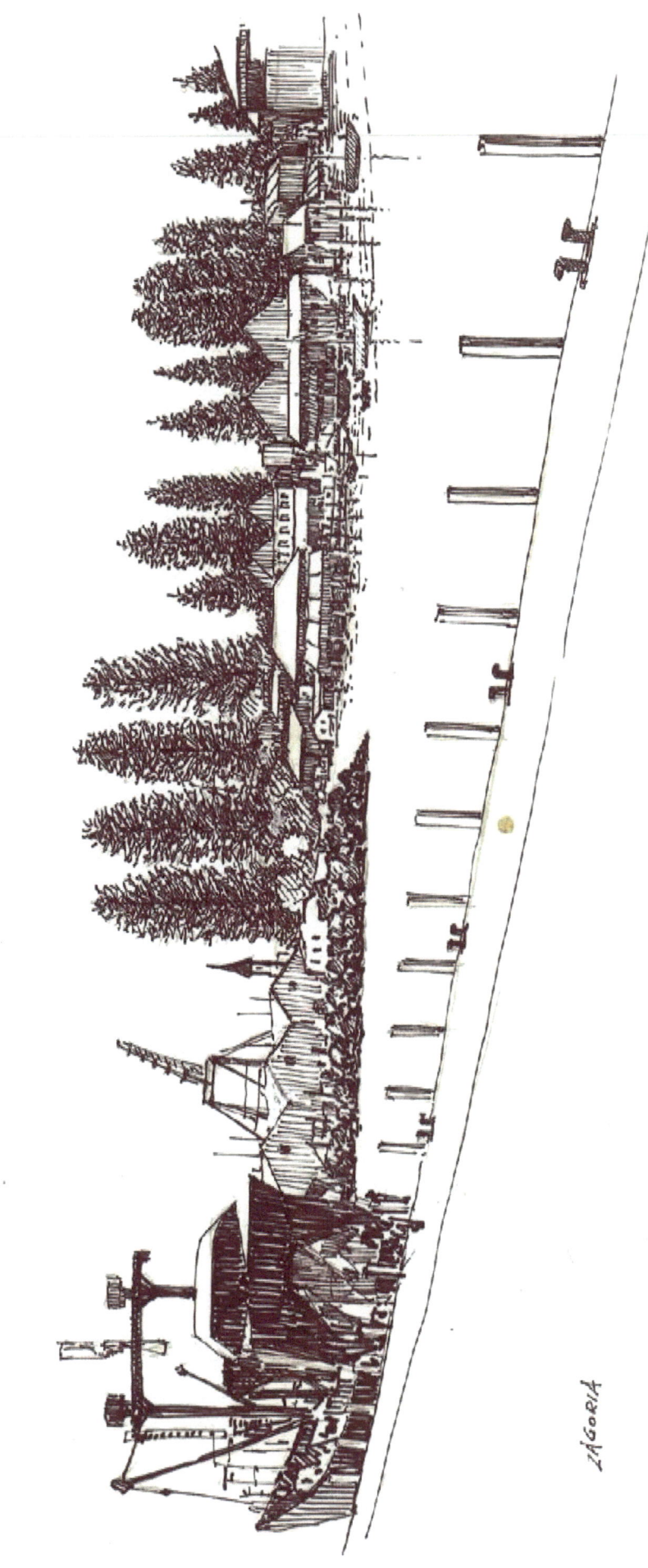

ZAGORIA

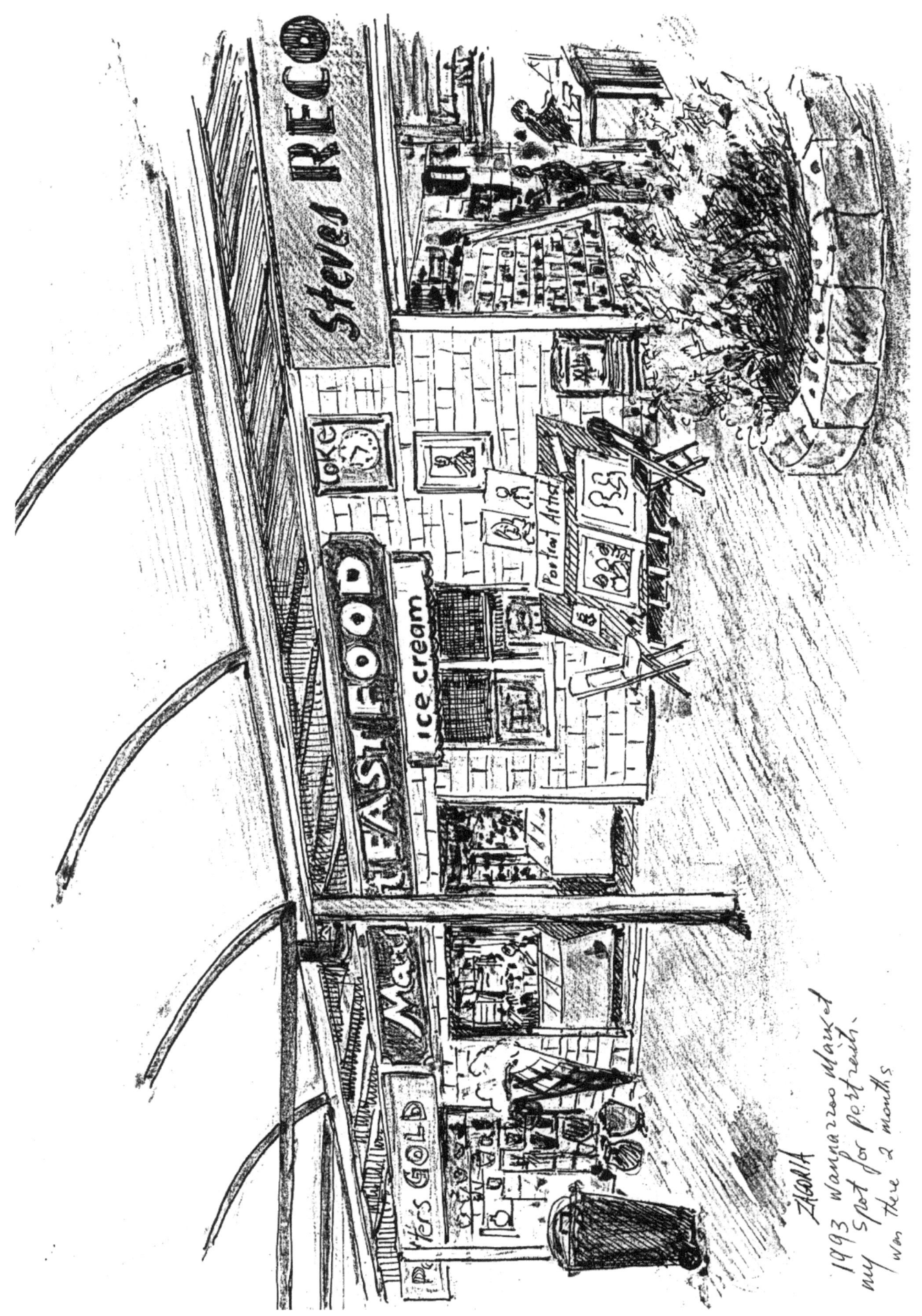

ZMONIA

1993 Wangaroo Market
my spot for portraits.
Won there 2 months

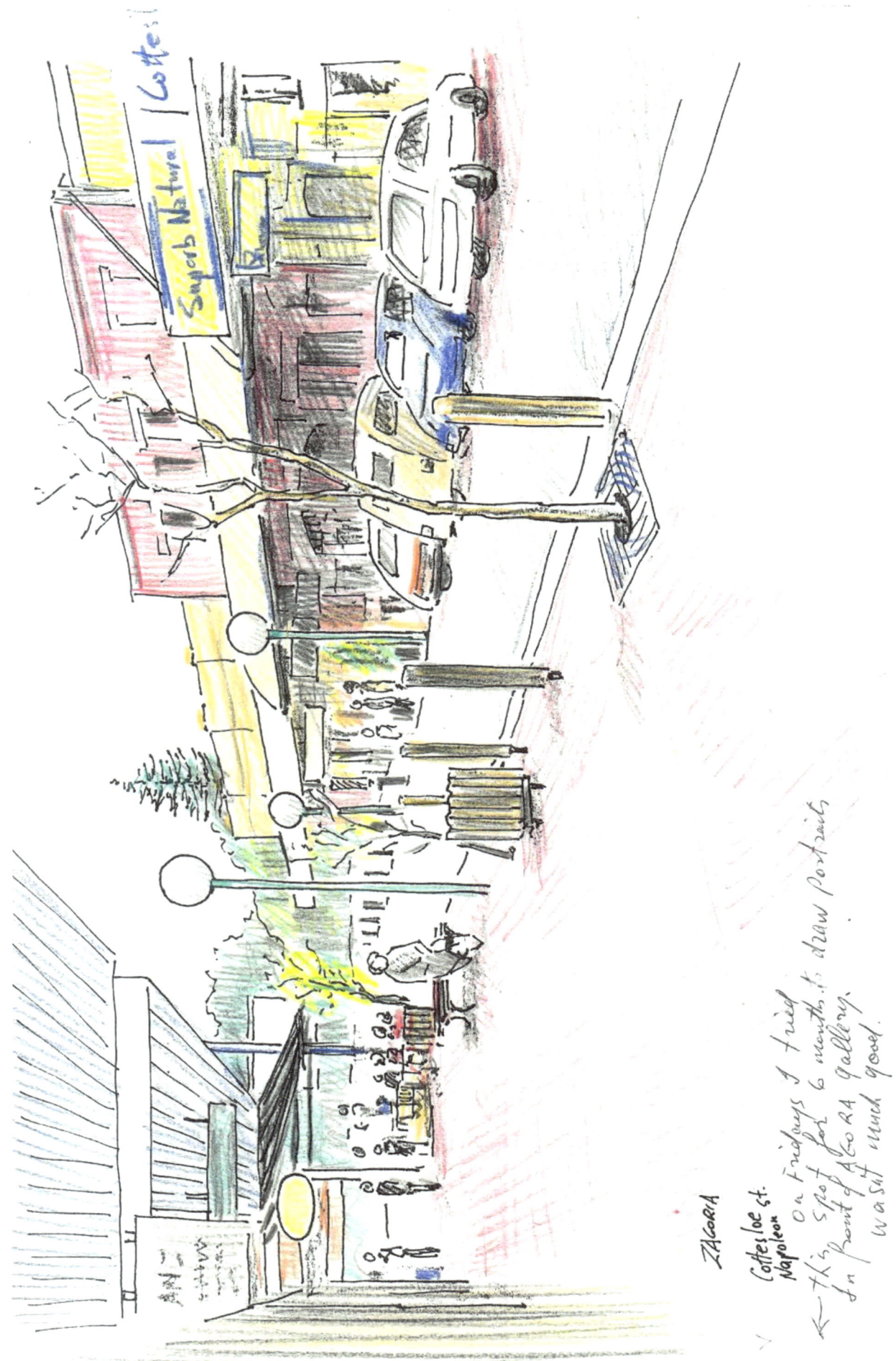

AGORA

Cottesloe St.
Napoleon

On Fridays I tried
this spot for 6 month. t draw Portraits
in front of AGORA galllery.
wasn't much good.

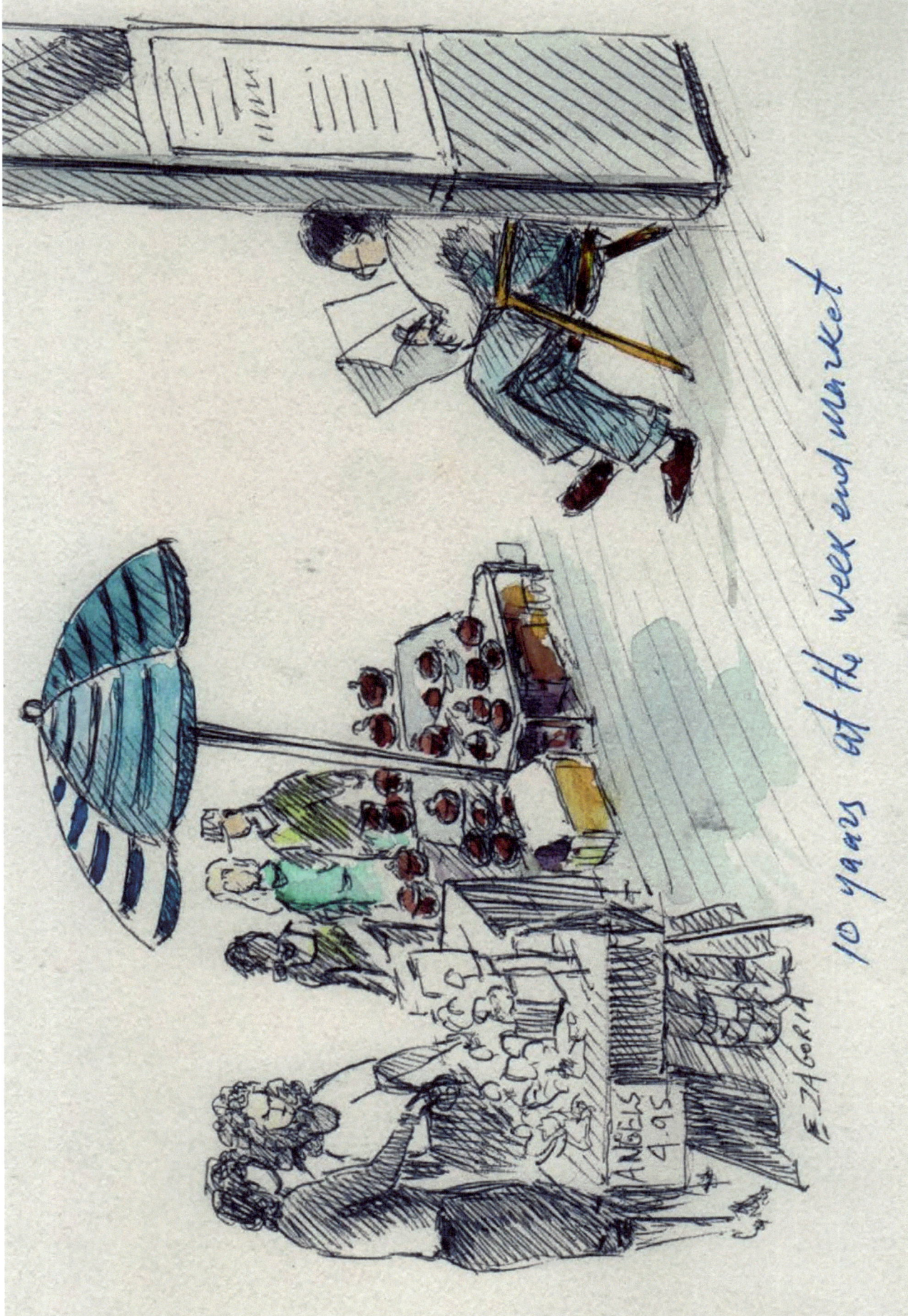

10 years at the week end market

E. ZAGORIA

ANGELS
4.95

ELI ZAGORIA, THE ARTIST (1922-2013)

Eli was born in 1922 in Riga, Latvia and at age 14 emigrated to South Africa. While still at school he was encouraged with his art.

After leaving school he served in the South African Army in the Medical Corp and was captured in Tobruk, and was a prisoner of war in Italy and Germany. There, in Stalag IVB, he met another artist who was British, and a prisoner of war too. He was Eli's first art teacher and told Eli he should take art up as a profession.

After returning to South Africa in 1946 he was given a full three year scholarship in the Art College in Johannesburg and then volunteered to go to Israel and join the Israeli Army in the 1949 War of Independence. In the Israeli Army he once again was in the medical corp helping the wounded and sick.

Eli married Estelle Kaplan in 1949 and they spent seven years in Israel and over 23 years in Zimbabwe before returning to Johannesburg for 13 years. During this time in Johannesburg he did portrait sketches at East Gate shopping centre.

Eli came to Perth in 1992. He has two sons Michael and Ilan born in Israel and a daughter Karen born in Zimbabwe.

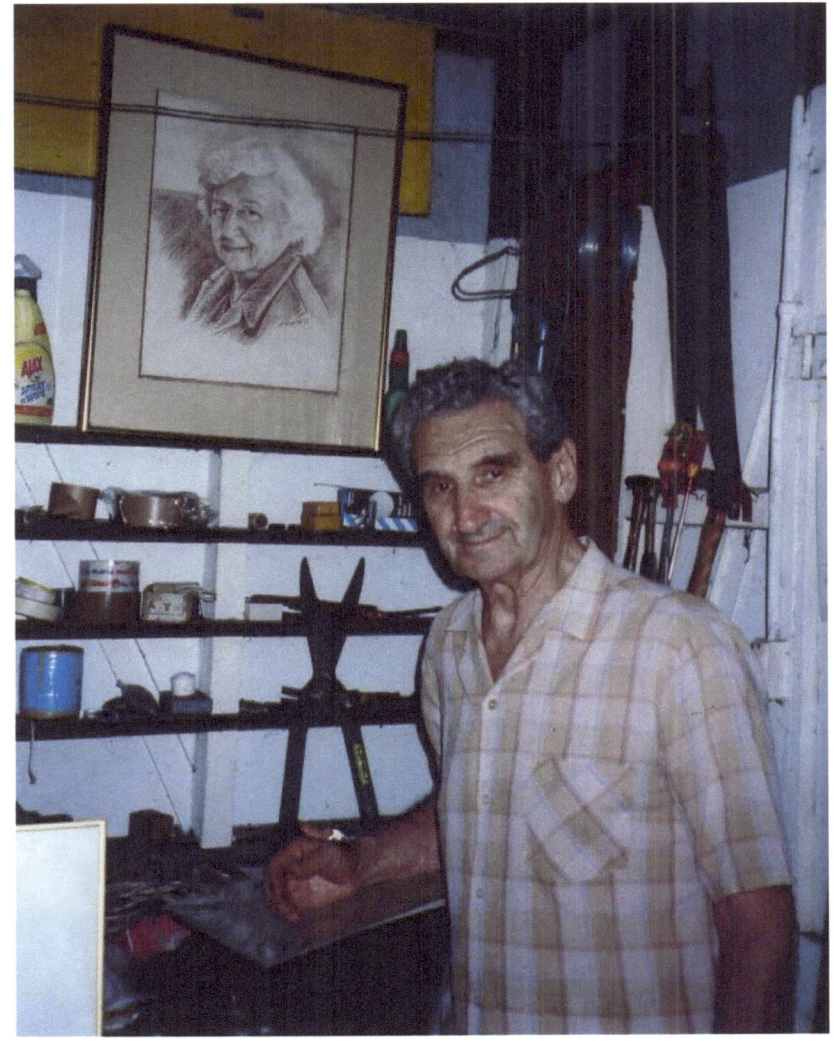

Eli, when he passed away early in 2013, still made his living from art, doing portraits and painting in his small studio at the back of his house. He estimated that he drew over 15,000 portraits over his lifetime.

Eli leaves behind his wife of 64 years, his three children and seven grandchildren.

*Eli in his studio
and workshop.*

*A portrait of his mother
hangs on the wall*

www.ingramcontent.com/pod-product-compliance
Lightning Source LLC
Chambersburg PA
CBHW040746200526
45159CB00023B/1752